T0149351

Latihan

A PATH TO THE GREAT LIFE AND A
NEW WAY TO PURIFY THE SOUL

ROZAK TATEBE

translated by Alana Simpson

BALBOA.
PRESS

A DIVISION OF HAY HOUSE

Balboa Press books may be ordered through booksellers or by contacting:

Balboa Press
A Division of Hay House
1663 Liberty Drive
Bloomington, IN 47403
www.balboapress.com.au
1 (877) 407-4847

Print information available on the last page.

ISBN: 978-1-5043-1812-9 (sc)
ISBN: 978-1-5043-1813-6 (e)

Balboa Press rev. date: 07/09/2019

CONTENTS

PROLOGUE

In June 1925, in Semarang, Central Java, Indonesia, a young man had a completely unexpected experience that eventually prompted him to found the movement called Subud. This movement has transformed the lives of hundreds of people around the world. Muhammad Subuh Sumohadiwidjojo was only 24 years old at this time. After he founded Subud, he become widely known as 'Bapak' and often referred to himself as such. 'Bapak' or 'Pa,' (meaning 'father') is not a special title in Indonesian but is normally used to address older men.

Subud has spread to 86 countries and all five continents. Despite this, most people have never even heard of Subud, and are often misinformed and confused about what it means. Subud members number not much more than 10,000 around the world. One reason for this could be many members find it hard to explain Subud to people who know nothing about it. A more likely reason is that Subud never proselytizes or advertises itself in an attempt to attract members. This is partly why I felt prompted to write this book, which you might say is a rash attempt at what is inherently impossible: to present a new message of Subud in its entirety. The views expressed in this book are my own and are based on my personal understanding of Subud's message.

The word 'latihan' is used frequently in Subud, and in this book. In Indonesian, the word means exercise, training, or workout. Subud has kept this word in the original Indonesian as no satisfactory translation was found. The word, 'kejiwaan' (meaning 'spiritual') is often added for clarification. In fact, the latihan is at the core of Subud and one of the central themes of this book. It refers to a state of spirituality where the functions of our mind—thoughts and emotions—are temporarily suspended by a power beyond that of humans. The essence of the latihan experience is direct contact with the Great Life, or the power of God the Creator of the entire universe. When people join Subud they access this contact through their own direct experience. This first contact is referred to as the 'opening.' They then become 'open' as will be explained later in the book.

It is my great hope that everyone who reads this book may have the chance to share this entirely new experience of self-development, and become truly aware of this enormous power of the Great Life Force.

Note: *'Subud' is the registered mark of the World Subud Association. The views and beliefs presented in this book are exclusively those of the author and cannot be construed as being those of the World Subud Association.*

PART I

What Is Subud?

1

THE ARRIVAL OF THE LATIHAN

The Spread of Subud

Subud spread around the world in 1956, partly due to the work of George Gurdjieff. Known as the foremost mystic of the twentieth century, Gurdjieff synthesized mystical and religious traditions from the past, including Greek Orthodox Christianity, Sufism, the Kabbalah of Judaism, Neoplatonism, Athenian Christianity, Pythagoreanism, Egyptian secret philosophies, and Buddhism;. To these, he added his own concepts, advocating a new spiritual and psychological training method that he called "the Work." This had a major international impact.

Though difficult to summarise briefly, the core concept of Gurdjieff's Work was that humans do not have access to their true selves and their true selves are still in a state of sleep. Because of this, our behaviour is subject to conditioning like that of a machine. We are incapable of doing something from our own initiative, and our words, beliefs, actions, and habits are all merely reactions to external stimuli and influence. We can only act in a mechanical way. The Work was a training in the development of consciousness.

When Peter D. Ouspensky, Gurdjieff's leading disciple, died in 1947, John G. Bennett, in the UK, became a leading exponent and teacher of the Gurdjieff method and headed a group of some hundreds of members. However, Bennet had difficulty developing the Work, not least because the elderly Gurdjieff had told him that after his death, someone would appear who would take over Gurdjieff's work and complete it. He also mentioned that the person was somewhere in the Malay Peninsula and already preparing for this task.

Bennett did not believe that Gurdjieff was to die soon nor that he would meet this promised new teacher in his lifetime. However, in 1956, Husein Rofé, the first Westerner to be opened in Subud in Indonesia returned to the UK, where he began to spread the word about Subud. Rofé had a firm conviction that this was his mission. Bennett met him and was intrigued by what he had to say. Not long after, Bennett decided to join. He himself said that his first experiences of the latihan shocked him. Despite his advanced knowledge of world religions and mystic traditions, this was something entirely different. Eventually, news of Subud spread from Bennett's followers to the international Gurdjieff network around the world. Throughout the 1950s and 1960s, Subud continued to grow with astonishing speed.

Bennett, Rofé and two or three new Subud members significant in the Gurdjeiff network, decided to invite Bapak to England. Unexpectedly, letters of invitation flooded in from other countries. Bapak's itinerary expanded to include England's major cities as well as the Netherlands, Switzerland, Germany, France, Norway, Italy, Spain, Greece and finally the West Coast of America. This journey took more than a full year and reinforced Subud's growth in the world.

Today, Subud has a presence in eighty-six countries. In fifty-four of these, Subud is run through national bodies, which, together, make up a global network called the World Subud Association (WSA).

However, while Subud exists in many countries, in relative terms, it has only a few members. One reason for this could be that Subud does not proselytize and it is difficult to put into words the meaning of the "latihan." Books about Subud do exist but many of them are personal memoirs of members' experiences with Bapak.

Of course, Subud is not the only experience that words are not adequate to explain. It is generally accepted that the "enlightenment" of Zen Buddhism is also indescribable, for example. Yet, hundreds of books have already been written about enlightenment using metaphors, and more continue to appear. Is the latihan of Subud something similar to this? Well, yes and no. While there are some similarities, the latihan is more radical.

Language is a tool that describes reality in this world and enables us to distinguish one thing from another. Yet even metaphors belong to the material world. Some metaphors prompt us to imagine and speculate on the reality of things *beyond* this world - but only by comparing them with things in the *known* world. This sort of speculation bears no relation to the latihan of Subud. To understand why, we need to return to and appreciate the unexpected experiences of that young twenty-four-year old Indonesian man.

Bapak's Childhood

Bapak wrote a brief autobiography in his later years, so we do have some information about his childhood. He lost his father at an early age and was brought up by his grandparents. He was an unusual child from early on. When still young, he would accompany his grandmother to weddings and there he would remark on whether the newlyweds were compatible or not. Any couples he had said were incompatible would end up divorcing or separated by the death of one partner. This happened so many times that eventually his grandmother and the rest of the family stopped taking him to weddings. He was also not able to speak ill of anyone or to use swear words. Even if he tried, his mouth would stop moving.

Bapak's beloved grandfather died when he was sixteen, which was a great shock to him. Around that time, he had a strange dream in which an old man dressed in black appeared, looking down at him from above. At that point, he thought he woke up but in the dream, the man told him that he had something important to say. "You will soon have to leave this place and work. God will call you back when you are thirty-two." Then, Bapak woke up in reality, but the man was nowhere to be seen. The dream had seemed too real to dismiss. He interpreted being called back to God at the age of thirty-two to mean he was going to die then. He had intended to study medicine, but to spend time doing so if he was going to die young seemed like a bad idea.

After much thought, he decided to give up the idea of becoming a doctor and in order to support his family, started to look for work. Fortunately, he was able to find full-time work in the railway station of the neighboring town. However, his heart was still heavy with the prediction that he would die at thirty-two. He had decided to study bookkeeping but work took up much of his time. Gradually, he became less satisfied with life and started visiting respected spiritual leaders in a search for the meaning of his existence.

In the ensuing years, Bapak changed jobs and locations a few times, while continuing to visit advanced spiritual teachers. His encounters with these teachers were unusual. None of them wanted to appear to be above him: one teacher called him 'master,' another said he had been waiting seventy years for him to come. An eighty-year-old teacher told him he could see that Bapak was enveloped in divine light and that he had nothing to teach him. Another teacher refused to make him his disciple and would only let him sit there, saying that in time, God would speak to Bapak directly.

With no satisfactory answers from these spiritual leaders, Bapak eventually lost his enthusiasm for spiritual exploration. He became more focused on real life in this world and devoted himself to the study of bookkeeping.

First Contact with the Great Life

Bapak often turned down visits from friends so he could concentrate on his studies. One night after midnight, he decided to take a walk as he was tired and needed a break. As he returned, his surroundings suddenly brightened and he looked up to see a sphere of light floating mid-air, shining like the sun. The sphere of light then entered his body from the top of his head, causing his entire body to shake ferociously. He thought he was having a heart attack and struggled back to his house so he could lie down in his bed, submit to God, and wait for his death.

Suddenly, his whole body had become transparent and was shining with an inner light. This continued for around thirty seconds. Then, without using his own will, he arose from his bed and his legs took him to the room that he used for study and prayer. He completed two rounds of Islamic prayers voicelessly. He returned to his room and was made to lie back in his bed and fall into a deep sleep. This marked his first contact with the powerful force of the latihan of Subud. Bapak called this power, "the Great Life."

This was not the end of Bapak's experience. The following day and the day after that, when he closed his eyes to try to sleep, his eyes would instead remain open and he would see everywhere into the distance. This made him fearful. The same force that he had encountered on the first night would manifest repeatedly, and, whether he willed it or not, move various parts of his body.

An Experience beyond Words

This experience continued for one thousand nights. Bapak got almost no sleep at night, but he continued to work as usual during the day. The movements of his body during these first latihan experiences were different every night.

One thousand nights of latihan is unthinkable for Subud members. After they are opened, they attend latihan regularly for thirty minutes at a time—and in principal, no more than twice or three times a week. Even with just this amount, their bodies will start to move, and changes gradually take place in their being. These effects are evidence of the immense power of the latihan. Bapak's experience of one thousand nights of intense latihan was extraordinary and suggests his significance in the eyes of God and the special intention God had for him.

The Movements of the Body in Latihan

The latihan of Subud is different from many other spiritual practices in that it does not require you to meditate where you are remote from others, such as a mountain retreat. Commitment to the latihan never requires one to live apart. Even as you live an ordinary life like everyone else, you do not sacrifice in any way the intensity or quality of the practice itself. Perhaps Bapak was made to physically experience these characteristics of the latihan with such intensity, it left him no room to doubt.

While in latihan, he found himself making many movements. In the beginning, he had no idea where these involuntary movements came from nor their meaning. All he knew was that some unknown force that prompted his body to move in different ways enveloped him. Some of the movements seemed to relate to the Indonesian self-defense art he had mastered in his youth; yet others were new techniques or a new kind of martial art that he had never come across before. At times, he was made to dance not only the Indonesian dances he was familiar with but also dances and steps from cultures and ethnic groups around the world. He would express himself vocally as well as sing. Over time, the quality of his voice improved and became more melodious.

All he could do was surrender his body to the movements that arose; there were no textbooks, guidelines, teachers, or coaches to explain things to him. It was an exercise in trust.

In fact, this is probably something we have all experienced at some time in our lives.

For example, children grow every day, but their pace of growth is slow. They often get impatient with this and want to grow up quicker—and even when you mark their growth on a wall or pillar one day and measure it again the next, there won't appear to be any difference in height. However, after a few months, it is clear that the child is definitely increasing in height. It is the same for everything that is alive and exists.

The Great Life Force of the universe continually works in this way, creating, growing, and sustaining life. Even just by living and eating, a child will grow. It happens without the need for explanation, and is accepted as fact. The great creative force of nature, a primordial universal power brings into being bacteria and organisms, animals and human beings over billions of years, is accepted as fact. Mountains erupt, valleys, lakes and rivers are created and the seasons change. These are the facts of nature. The changes that occur in us as we practice the latihan happen unconsciously over time in a similar way. When Bapak received the latihan, it was in this way - close to that of the great force of nature, and he readily submitted to it. He was not sure about it in the beginning, but guessed that the force working within him was one higher than human knowledge and one that it was right to submit to.

After repeated experiences like this, and through his own discernment, Bapak eventually understood the meaning and purpose of the movements that took place in his latihan. Based on this understanding, he emphasized two aspects in particular: the connection between the movements that people made in latihan and their process of purification, and the understanding that these movements were also a manifestation of their worship of God.

As will become clear in the next chapter, when one is in a latihan state, the mind is stilled and thoughts and emotions are suppressed, however, there is no loss of awareness or clouding of consciousness. One remains fully conscious and always aware of what is happening.

THE WORSHIP OF GOD
AND PURIFICATION

Standing on One's Own Feet

Subud does not have ideas, teachings, or doctrines in the way that religions do. Nobody pays attention to the religion or creed of other members. As Subud members who practice the latihan regularly are aware, it is experience-based rather than doctrine-based. Subud members often judge right and wrong, and make decisions about their lives based on what they each feel and experience in the latihan. Oftentimes, people who do follow a religion find their understanding of their religion deepens as they progress in the latihan.

Sometimes, if members have questions about their practice of the latihan, they will seek advice from more experienced members. However, this advice simply presents points of reference; only the person him/herself can ultimately decide what is right. In no way do Subud members depend on the advice of so-called leaders or superior spiritual advisers. Some people firmly believe that they need to follow a guru in order to achieve enlightenment. However, the follower may never truly become independent of the guru.

With Subud, you stand and walk through life on your own feet. This is the gift you receive from the power beyond knowing. Subud will not work for people who want to depend on someone else to help them live their lives.

The Functions of the Mind and Inner Feeling

Can we say that Subud is an entirely new experience hitherto unavailable to human beings, and what does this mean?

We can say this because it gives us a new understanding of the two major functions of the human mind: thought and emotion. Thoughts and emotions do not have mass or shape; they cannot be readily studied by science. There is no proof as to whether they are matter or anti-matter. Most people believe that our cerebral cortex, which enables thoughts and feelings, is what elevates us amongst living things and differentiates us from animals.

It has taken several millions of years for humans to evolve from apes to where we are today. The history of this evolution is not clear, but in the process, we learned that our organs and functions of the human body get stronger and more efficient the more they are used, while the less they are used, the weaker they become. Thoughts and emotions are functions of the human body, and therefore it follows that this principle applies to them, also.

Bapak said that these thoughts and emotions are there so that we can understand this world and live under its conditions. Our ability to distinguish between objects and analyze their properties, to imagine and discover efficient ways to use them are dependent on our thoughts and emotions. Little wonder human beings have put most of their efforts into developing those functions. Civilization and our current lifestyles are the outcomes of these efforts.

Bapak stated that this came about because the conditions of this world are in continual flux, and most human beings can't help but be influenced by these constant changes in response to them. As the sciences advanced, the development of the mind was forefront and gradually, our spiritual sense—our inner feeling—fell away from that realm of inner peace and into the realm of thought. Humans were no longer governed by the calmness of the inner feelings. Everything became subject to thought rather than feeling. These days, our emotions and minds are continually busy, and we rarely have the opportunity to be at peace.

Bapak pointed out that while thoughts and emotions are essential functions that enable us to live our lives; they are useless when it comes to understanding God or spiritual matters. Human beings were given a different function to help them contact the spiritual world: an innate inner feeling. This inner feeling gives expression to our soul and if our soul is alive, we can connect to the spiritual world. If we are only working from our thoughts and emotion, our souls are asleep. They are like the seeds of a plant that cannot germinate because the soil is not ready. If the soul does not awaken, it cannot grow and expand its functions as we live in the world. Our inner feelings have become weakened and their function substantially reduced. We cannot feel nor consider the power of God or the existence of a universe governed by God. We cannot even remember that we are God's creation and that we are connected to God and the spiritual universe through our souls.

The latihan allows us to restore contact with the Great Life and awaken our true human soul. We need to think about how this relates to where we are now in the world

The Latihan Experience and the Worship of God

In nature, phenomena occur without explanation. The changes that occur in latihan follow this pattern. If you truly pay attention to the movements of your body in latihan, you can come to know what they mean, as Bapak was able to. While Bapak was a Muslim, the forms of prayer he found himself doing in latihan were not confined to Islamic forms of prayer. Through these repeated experiences, he came to realize that the movements of his latihan were not just exercises but they held a deep significance.

With patience, you will see that your movements too change over time. You will see how the rougher movements you made at the beginning become more refined. Movements that were seemingly random start to have meaning, such as forms of prayer, or expressions of yourself. The challenge is to persist patiently with your latihan until the stage when these changes are understood (this will be covered in detail in the section on Purification). This type of progress is not measurable by ordinary means and can take several years.

To surrender to the power that works through the latihan is to respect that power and submit unconditionally to it. This power is the Great Life force that comes directly from God, and the latihan itself becomes an act of venerating God, following God and worshipping God. Through this worship of God, we receive what is necessary for ourselves. This is the purpose and the essence of the latihan. Members who have been doing the latihan for a long time understand what this means - not because Bapak said it was so but because they reached this conclusion through their own experiences.

The latihan is neither religion nor doctrine but can only be understood through first-hand experience. This truth limits how we explain this content to others. We can only use words—no matter how inadequate—to express some of the reality of this experience so that people can imagine it for themselves. Books have been written in an attempt to express this; however, their contents are immediately misinterpreted as religious doctrine or teachings.

Bapak suggested that the human race had lived in an age of faith until the arrival of the modern era and that Subud was now the gateway to a new era of spiritual experience. In the age of faith, there was no way of objectively demonstrating the content of spiritual matters or beliefs. The latihan ushered in a new era whereby anyone can verify his or her own beliefs through direct experience. Whenever we experience something, our mind—that is to say, our thoughts and emotions—inevitably interferes and has an impact on the content of that experience. It is like trying to discern the scenery outside by looking through frosted glass or a veil. In the latihan, because we are not subject to the influence of our hearts and minds and our thoughts and our emotions, there is no interference with our direct apprehension of the spiritual universe.

As Bapak indicated, using thought or emotion to access the spiritual universe creates interference and hampers our understanding of it. We live in a world that requires us to use our thoughts and emotions every moment of the day until we die. A scientific materialist viewpoint assumes that God or the supernatural cannot exist because it is impossible to perceive God or God's power in this world. Even in ancient times, spiritual seekers knew that thoughts and emotions interfered with spiritual understanding and so they devised methods of meditation requiring effort and ingenuity to minimize this interference. Even so, they had to start from the power of thought and emotion while striving to minimize them. They had to use the force of willpower to suppress troublesome thoughts and subdue unruly emotions.

Some meditation methods use mind focus – such as on sounds or images - to suppress thought. For example, Zen meditation uses breath control to help induce a state of emptiness (*mu*). Yoga is also fundamentally a type of meditation. Hatha Yoga involves a variety of poses that are about creating a calm state of mind to promote meditation.

These physically challenging solutions, however, do not solve some fundamental issues. It is true the will has a controlling power and can therefore suppress thoughts and emotions to some extent. However, this is not because willpower is something separate from thoughts, emotions, and desires but because it is *the same* as them. In fact, it serves the core function of initiating these thoughts and emotions. Humans were furnished with willpower for the same reason and purpose they have thoughts and emotions: to explore the limitations and the nature of the heterogeneous world outside ourselves and to improve our own lives in this world.

To use the will to discover the spiritual world beyond this one is not only futile, but actually gets in the way. Willpower cannot leap above the limitations and conditions of this world and lead us to God or to the spiritual reality governed by God's power. Using willpower to suppress interference from thoughts and emotions can have the opposite effect. It can produce unmoving, strong-willed people who may be able to witness visions of Buddha and other mysterious phenomena but perhaps may actually be seeing simply the projections of their will and illusions that have nothing to do with spiritual reality.

Impurities of the Character and Mind

Purification means to clean something that is dirty. When our skin is soiled, we wash it clean in a bath or shower. The dirt we purify in latihan is not the dirt or soiling of our bodies, but the dirt, or defects in our inner selves. What is the nature of this dirt? Jesus Christ said that 'It's not what goes into your mouth that defiles you; you are defiled by the words that come out of your mouth. [Matthew 15:11 NLT][3] Our inner selves are damaged by the negative energy generated by thoughts and emotions in the form of anger, hatred, jealousy, desire, cruelty, or feeling superior/inferior, or indifferent to others. Once the energy from an angry outburst has dispersed and faded, we forget about it, even if it has hurt someone else. However, it does not end there. Any residual negative energy that has not fully dispersed penetrates us, tainting our senses, our feelings, and our thoughts, then eventually contaminating our mind and body. A couple who argue furiously but make up quickly with no bad feelings can dissolve this residual energy so that it does not hang over them. However, as we go about our everyday lives, we do not even imagine that this process goes on internally. We have lost the power to feel what happens inside of us.

The human body is engineered to have a precise awareness of the world for optimal use in our everyday lives. Our eyes, nose and mouth are all connected to the outside. Our eyes are endowed with an extraordinary ability to perceive the world, yet we cannot see what is inside of us. It is the same with our ears. Our thoughts and emotions, cannot apprehend our inner state, nor understand the spiritual world that transcends this one. Humans have relied on power of our thoughts and emotions for everything and it has become harder to search for spiritual truth. We were quick to develop our thoughts and emotions, but our inner feelings, which were supposed to regulate their activities, became weaker in the process.

A Training like No Other

The latihan is different from other forms of training. In latihan, we temporarily suppress the power of our thoughts and emotions and set aside our consciousness—something that humans cannot achieve through effort or willpower. We can only do this with the help of a transcendent power. Most people do not believe that achieving such a state is possible to begin with. Therefore, they also find it hard to believe that in latihan they can suddenly have direct experience of spiritual truth and the power of God.

Subud does not insist that this entirely new state of awareness is correct or that you must believe it. Subud only states that anyone who so wishes is free to test this truth for themselves. Remember that Bapak said we have shifted from the age of faith to the age of experience, from the experience of the physical world to the experience of the spiritual world that exists in the realm of the supernatural. Until now, people had no way of concretely ascertaining the truth of their spiritual awareness except by anchoring it in their own beliefs. This gave rise to superstitions and proverbs such as the belief that miracles only happen to those who believe in them. With the latihan, people can have this experience and verify its authenticity directly for themselves.

This is not the only reason why the latihan is a form of training that is unparalleled, nor does it fully explain how the latihan works. For the state of latihan to emerge and do its work, it is a required condition that our soul is awakened, and its function restored.

As mentioned earlier, our souls, enveloped in the forceful pressure of this world, are in a state of sleep. The human soul is a bridge that connects us to the spiritual universe and it has the important role of checking on our lives in this world, and at times, communicating information or suggestions to us. (Note that in some cases, and as I explain later, instead of being filled with the true human life force, the soul is filled with the lower forces that have entered that person. Even in these cases, the soul can manipulate the body as though from a command center.) The life force of the true human soul is a force that is of a higher order than the ordinary human life force, as it is aware of things beyond the grasp of our mind, such as our direction and purpose in life. Needless to say, the soul cannot fulfill this role if it is in a state of sleep.

A Negative Inheritance

Purification involves another challenge. The process involves not just the purification of our own mistakes, but the faults and defects that we, as descendants, have ultimately inherited from our parents, grandparents and even our ancestors before that. We inherit some of our physical characteristics from our parents; some are advantageous to us and some are not, such as propensities to certain illnesses. In the same way, our mental disposition is partially inherited from our parents who inherited some of personalities from their ancestors. Considering this trail, it is no wonder that we carry a psychological inheritance that has piled up inside us but is not part of us, and that unfortunately, is mostly negative rather than positive. If our ancestral inheritance had been more positive than negative, we could have expected improvements in humanity over the ages and the creation of a modern society that is close to ideal. Instead, we have negative energies created by human emotions and thoughts, driven by desires that manifest as anger, hatred, jealousy, self-centeredness, combative impulses, and feelings of superiority or inferiority.

In physics, the law of the conservation of energy means that once formed, energy can never dissipate completely. When heated, the energy of water transforms into the energy of steam, and this water vapor becomes the kinetic energy that can power vehicles. The energy itself changes state but does not vanish. Energy that is generated by the feelings and emotions is similar. Regardless of whether the energy is positive or negative, the person at which it is directed will react by producing another energy internally. If the subject is a sensitive person, they will be able to feel this. Moreover, even if the negative energy produced weakens and dissipates, the residue always remains, attaching itself to the mind and accumulating as dirt. This will end up degrading that person's mind and character, making further generations of negative energy more likely. While this may not immediately manifest as illness, it is the same as psychological stress. Everything seems fine in the beginning, but as the stress builds up over time, it eventually causes severe physical and mental disorders.

Bapak described mental disorders as more serious than physical illnesses because a physical illness largely only affects the person with the condition, whereas someone who has defects of temperament and personality can cause unhappiness to hundreds, even thousands of people. Most people ignore or are unaware of the defects they inherit from their ancestors. These become habits, which they don't want to lose. Bapak knew that the latihan is a process that removes the impurities that do not belong to us and restores us to our original selves.

However, such a process of thorough purification attempts to remake us from the ground up and requires and a great deal of work. First, we purify our bodies, and then progressively, this work penetrates to our inner selves to purify our emotions, thoughts, and consciousness. Bapak underwent this entire process himself, and generally, people in Subud undergo a slower, step-by-step process. It is impossible to say how long this might take. The quality and quantity of impurities each person has accumulated in their inner selves vary. How strong they are internally to withstand the changes that occur through the purification also varies.

The Resurrection of the Body and Mind

I wrote earlier that the experience of the latihan is the contact with the Great Life, which flows through the mind and body to purify each part. What does this actually mean? Bapak expressed it as 'the resurrection of the mind and body.'

Our physical bodies are alive from the moment we are born. Thus, the resurrection that Bapak talks about is not of this world but as seen from the perspective of the spiritual world. It is as though our physical bodies do not yet have a spiritual life; spiritually, they are dead. In other words, our bodies do not yet have the spiritual bodies that will form the foundation for our life in the world beyond.

Japan's state broadcaster, NHK, recently produced eight episodes of a series showcasing advanced medical research from around the world. The content made a significant impact not just on viewers but also amongst experts in the medical community. For example, until now, the assumption was that the body was controlled by the brain, which acted as its command center. Researchers, such as Nobel prize winning Shingo Yamanaka and heart specialist Kenji Samukawa, used advanced optical ultrasound imagining technology to show how organs inside the human body cross-transmit messages without waiting for instructions from the brain.[4] This suggests the existence of a vast, communication network inside the human body that allows the organs to send messages to each other.

Bapak had already suggested something very like this new discovery. While he was concerned with the spiritual body rather than the material body, he did say that each body part has a role preordained by God. When our bodies come alive through the influx of the Great Life, these parts will be able to access instructions on how to fulfill that role rather than have to be instructed by us (our brains).

The Great Life enters our bodies through our soul and, as Bapak said, our bodies are introduced to our souls. Before that, the parts and organs of our body were not aware of the existence of the human soul. When the Great Life flows into us with the power of the soul, these parts become aware for the first time and recognize that the soul is our true master. What this means is that, for example, if someone's legs are completely purified and filled with the Great Life, those legs become more than a physical part of the body. When the owner of those legs walks down the street and doesn't see something that would cause them to trip, their legs automatically stop them before they become aware of the hazard themselves. If someone's eyes have become purified, when he or she meets someone, they know without thinking, what the caliber of that person is by just by looking at them. Should that person be harmful, his or her eyes will naturally look away. If the person they meet is a wise, courteous person, his or her eyes will open wider to look at them. The same goes for the ears (hearing) and other parts of the body. Bapak expected all Subud members to experience this eventually. Members who have not experienced this level of purification, can use testing (explained in Part II, The

Gift of Testing) to help them understand and feel this reality for themselves.

People just starting with their latihan should not assume that the benefits of this form of purification come easily. There are obstacles to overcome at every level of purification and conditions that come with it.

3

BAPAK'S MISSION

Spreading the Latihan

One evening, after latihan, while Bapak was seated and performing *zikir* (devotional Islamic prayers), suddenly a massive book that looked like an atlas, fell into his lap. He opened the book and on the first page was a picture of a robed man with a description written in Arabic beneath it. The letters transformed into the Roman alphabet and he read, "Prophet Muhammad, Messenger of God." After he had finished reading it, the robed man appeared to nod and smile. Bapak was astonished.

When he turned to the following page, there was a picture of people of different races. They started to move to their own rhythm as if they were all alive. The third page also had a picture of people like the one before, and here the people were alive and moving and talking; some were in prayer, some were crying and calling on God to forgive their sins. Bapak's amazement deepened and he shut the book and hugged it to his chest. At that moment, the book disappeared, leaving him only with a sense of confusion and the feeling of the weight of the book against him.

After some time, he had another experience while he was doing *zikir* after latihan. Again, at this time, a thick book suddenly landed in his lap. He opened it only to find that while there were hundreds of pages, they were all blank. Then words started forming on the first page. They read, "This book will only be written in if a question is asked." He was taken aback but decided to surrender completely to God and boldly ask the purpose and use of the book he had received before and what would happen to him in the years to come. The answer then appeared in the book. "The illustrations in that book were to show you that it will be your duty to awaken those people who wish to repent of all their sins before Almighty God and who wish to surrender to God with a feeling of patience, submission, and acceptance."

Bapak asked several other questions. In one of the answers he received, he was told there would be a great war after which Java and the other islands would be released from Dutch rule. When that happened, it would be his duty to travel around the world and spread the latihan.

Bapak was neither happy nor excited when he read this. He felt completely powerless and racked with remorse over his helplessness before God. Tears flowed from his eyes. He asked, "How can I, who is ignorant, poor and lacking in knowledge, achieve such a thing?" The answer came. "You must have faith in this revelation. Almighty God has power in all things and He is the creator of the universe and all that is within it."

Like the one before it, the book then disappeared from his lap. Later, it felt to him as though the contents of this book had somehow been absorbed and become part of his inner feelings. From that time on, whenever he had a question, all he had to do was to put it to his inner self and the answer would appear.

The events that the book had predicted came to pass, including World War II and Indonesia's liberation from the Netherlands, The prediction that Bapak would take a world trip was also to come true, albeit twenty years later, in 1957

Later, Bapak made frequent trips around the world, opening people who so wished, and explaining the significance of the latihan. In the process, he gave many talks aimed at Subud members, which are a precious legacy and a vital source of information for all members. These talks are available to people after they have experienced the latihan and are not openly published to avoid confusion.

The latihan of Subud is not something that Bapak came up with himself. It is from a source that transcends the human. Bapak firmly stated that he was not the creator of the latihan nor was he a special person like the prophets from ancient times. He considered the latihan as a gift from God to all humankind, and hoped that members would reveal its value and significance.

'What comes from God, returns to God,' as the saying goes. God is infinite and the universe is boundless. Therefore, it is not surprising that there are countless paths back to God that are almost infinitely far and take an almost infinite amount of time.

Once, Bapak apparently told members that while the speed of light is faster than anything in this world, it still takes eight minutes and twenty seconds for it to travel from the sun to Earth. Angels can travel a thousand times faster than light, but it still takes them one hundred years to travel to the edge of the Universe and return to God. It would take seventy million years for humans to reach God. However, God placed a part of His essence in his creatures so that if He wills it, they can reach God much faster. Jesus and the Prophet Muhammad also spoke about this. Only God can create the way to perfection in this life and the way back to Him. All that is required of us is to be willing to let go of everything and simply surrender to God and accept His will.

The Ascension Experience

As mentioned earlier, when he was younger, Bapak had had a dream wherein a man told him that God would call him when he was thirty-two. Bapak had already looked for answers to this mysterious prediction from several famous wise men but none of them could give him an answer.

He was to discover that what happened to him at the age of thirty-two was not his *physical* death, but a journey of ascension beyond the stars to the spiritual universe. This ascension was close to that experienced by Jesus, and the Prophet Muhammad. During this experience, Bapak's soul and consciousness left the earth and our sun's Milky Way galaxy, and journeyed through the seven levels of the universe. The contact with the Great Life that Bapak had been given at the age of twenty-four was a new gift from God for the benefit of humankind. He was informed that it was his mission to spread the latihan to everyone and to bring the contact with the Great Life to people around the world. Below is Bapak's description of his experience as written in his autobiography:

"At once, I felt myself lengthen, widen and expand into a sphere, and I felt myself suddenly released from some great object, like a jewel being freed from its setting. I then found myself in a great space. Far before me was a group of stars like diamonds in an earring. I asked myself what this was and received the reply that what I saw was the universe that I had left. I assumed that I was dead, so I kept saying, "Allahu Akbar, Allahu Akbar, Allahu Akbar"—God is Almighty, God is Almighty, God is Almighty.

Then with great speed, I traveled across a huge expanse. Before me, I could see mountain-like cones of light, seven them, stacked one above the other, and each connected by a cord of brilliant white light. I approached the first cone and entered it. Within could be seen a vast panorama, much greater than that I had seen before."[1]

He progressed toward the first and second cone-shaped mountains and when he had reached the sixth, he felt completely powerless. He was raised up into the seventh cone-shaped mountain but had no idea of where he should turn or how to move forward. All he could do was say, 'Allah, Allah.' He had the strange experience whereby he could see everything no matter how far away, as though it was in front of his own eyes. He mentioned that he could see his son asleep and half-falling out of his bed, for example.

Bapak talks about this experience in his autobiography but does not describe everything that he had experienced. To do so, he felt, might invite misunderstanding.

A Conversation about the Great Life

In his book, *Subud*, Robert Lyle quotes from a fascinating conversation between Bapak and a Catholic monk that took place during Bapak's first world trip. An excerpt is included below:

How did Bapak become aware that he was in contact with the Great Force of Life?
Bapak had an intimate experience. He can say nothing about the source of this experience. Only God knows if it was a revelation. Bapak can affirm that he does not compare himself with anyone— with a prophet, for example. He only knows what he himself has experienced. He followed that which was indicated to him, because he felt that it was the will of God that he should do so, and this implies nothing that goes beyond the experience itself.

In speaking of the Great Force of Life, Bapak refers to a reality that is not included in our Western categories. What is the nature of this Great Force?
It is not God, but a primordial creature. It is that force which conveys into the creation the divine ordinances, or the commandments of God.

Is the Force of Life to be regarded as a person? Can one speak of it in the depths of one's heart, or is it an impersonal principle?
The Great Force of Life is not personal. It penetrates everything that exists, from the purest essence to the coarsest matter. The Great Force of Life is not a separate being, such as, for example, the Pure Soul, that of the seventh degree which can neither touch nor be touched by matter, but the Great Force of Life enters everywhere.[2]

As is evident from the above and in other conversations with Bapak, while he declared that the latihan was a gift and a grace from God, he never once described it as a Divine Revelation. It was his understanding that the latihan of Subud was a shorter and quicker way back to God. He believed that contact with the power of God had always existed as a human right that was lost due to our own mistakes, and that the contact with the Great Life through the latihan was a way to help us exercise this right. This builds a pathway for the soul to return to God—or rather, reconstructs the lost pathway. Bapak passed away in 1987 but this pathway for the sleeping soul to awaken is still available to anyone.

Subud is both radical and innovative. As a writer and someone who has been practicing the latihan for many years, I truly hope that someday, people will recognize its value even though that day may still be a long way off.

4

THE SPIRITUAL UNIVERSE

The Visible and Invisible Universe

The latihan is of the realm governed by the Great Life and only occurs when thoughts and emotions are put aside. In the realm of the Great Life, neither thoughts nor emotions hold sway. The effects of the latihan are brought about by the changes that take place organically inside each person. These changes are not the result of a Subud theory or idea.

Spiritual truth is like the noonday star; it exists but is invisible and hidden from this world. Everyone knows that brightness of the sky in daytime obscures the light of the stars. The sky is bright because the moisture and innumerable particles of fine dust and debris floating in the atmosphere reflect and scatter light. It is a scientific truth that our sight improves as our surroundings get brighter due to the presence of these impurities.

In the same way, spiritual truth exists but is hidden from our ordinary eyes and understanding this is a transformative experience. The dazzle of our thoughts and emotions, made bright by the impurities within us, has blinded us to the true state of the universe. If we realize this, we can start to see truth in a new way. We can become aware of a vast, spiritual universe expanding to many times the size of our visible, material universe.

This understanding of Bapak's might appear radical. Until science progresses enough to explain fully how our thoughts and emotions work, it cannot be proved or disproved. Scientific theories of the brain's visual function do not contradict Bapak's concept so much as partially support it; for example, the theory that the brain's visual cortex receives electromagnetic stimuli from light. By recognizing the patterns and shapes of these stimuli, it forms a map of the world within the brain. As our eyes see only this map of the world from within our brains, who can say it is the true universe.

The assertion that Subud is an experience and not a religion is not based on logic or interpretation, but on a more profound spiritual reason at its core. The inner feelings of a person must be in an untroubled and pure state before they can perceive the existence of the Great Life. As long as the mind's functions are at work—even by a small amount—they will stir up and muddy the inner feelings, and conceal the spiritual world from them and make it seem as though it had never existed. Only when the functions of the mind are fully stopped can the awareness of this spiritual world become possible. Normally, this can only be experienced after you have passed through the gates of death.

Bapak's Cosmology

Bapak's understanding of the spiritual universe was that it consists of seven layers of life force worlds. The seven layers of the universe are shown below, in order from lowest to highest:

The world of the material life force
The world of the vegetable life force
The world of the animal life force
The world of the ordinary human life force
The world of Rohani (the world of the life force of humans who have reached a state of completeness)
The world of Rachmani (life force higher than that of Rohani)
The world of Rabani (life force higher than that of Rachmani)

Each of these seven worlds exist independently, but the lower four—material, vegetable, animal, ordinary human—exist both within us and outside of us humans. They enter us through our mothers, through what we eat, and in other ways. The life force contained in food is a spiritual energy and does not die when it is cooked. These life forces are important elements that make up the human body and are active night and day. They both sustain our bodies and support our lives on this earth. Our awareness, emotions and thoughts would not operate efficiently without the help of these four lower forces. All living creatures, including humans, must eat, since we deplete energy through our activities and must replenish this energy with food. We can also derive much pleasure from eating delicious foods. Of all four lower forces, only the ordinary human life force enters us through sexual union and not through the consumption of food.

These forces are like assistants, or partners, that participate in our physical activities in order to aid us in living our lives as true humans. If we did not have the material life force inside of us, we would probably not be able to recognise material things for what they are or know their properties. This, in turn, allow us to build necessities such as houses, clothes, equipment and machinery. If the vegetable life force did not exist inside of us, we would not be able to take in energy through food, then grow, and sustain our

30

bodies. We are mostly made up of vegetable elements. Likewise, without the animal elements inside of us, we would not possess sufficient courage and passion to face challenges; we would also lack patience and perseverance. The ordinary human life force helps us to lead a life that is different from that of animals.

The Lower Life Forces and Their Influence

The lower four life forces hold particular significance for human beings. This is because most of our bodily functions occur with the cooperation of these forces; they are integrated within us, and participate in—as well as exert—a strong influence over the activities of our heads and hearts. The planet we live on is unique. Even in the Milky Way, no planet has been found with a material environment that nurtures plants, animals, humans and other creatures above the material level, while coexisting with the higher life forces.

The world of the ordinary human life force is positioned right in the middle of the seven life forces and acts as a bridge between the life forces below the human and those that are above. Therefore, at the same time, they are pulled up towards the forces above them and dragged down to the forces below them. In order for humans to live in a material world, we were given material bodies that consist of the four life forces below the human, while on the other hand; we also have souls that contain the Rohani life force.

The material world, which is at the bottom, is the one inhabited by humans. Here, we are isolated from other worlds by the barrier of death. If the universe is a limited expression of God's nature, the material world is the narrowest, lowest form of expression of this. Here, there are many restrictions and laws to maintain order. For example, without the laws of chemistry and physics, chaos would prevail. My own opinion is that the material world requires so many rules because of its lower standing in the universe.

Matter can exist almost indefinitely in the material world, which is its home. However, matter cannot move autonomously; it can only move when it is being moved. Even when it is being moved, it can only do so in a strictly predetermined direction and method. There is no room for self-will in that movement. Moreover, unlike the plants, animals and humans that exist above it, matter has absolutely no consideration of others, nor is it alive and capable of expressing will. Matter does not care how many thousands of people may die because of a volcanic eruption or a tsunami. For matter, there is no cruelty; that's just its viewpoint. Maybe material things do have thought, but if so, the content is far removed from that of human beings.

The human soul is not material but as creatures that have been created on earth, we have to obey the laws of this world. Nevertheless, we often feel limited by them and lacking in freedom. If God is the creator of this universe and is love itself, we might question why He created such an absurd world. According to Bapak, this would be a complete misunderstanding. God did not make the material world as Heaven, but as the lowest-level world. So rather than ask why did God make such a world, what we should ask is why should humans, who are not matter, have to live in such a world. It is possible that therein lies the reason that humans thirst so much for freedom, because, in reality, the higher we climb in the order of the universe, the freer we become.

Bapak mentioned that there is an affinity between the material life force and our thinking. People make use of the properties and rules of matter to build objects necessary for our lives. As we manipulate matter, our thinking absorbs some of the properties of these material objects and is affected by them. We start to hold affection for the things we have created ourselves. Some people become obsessed with these objects and start to rely on them rather than on God. Money symbolises the material, and for these people, wealth becomes the object of their worship. Matter is entirely uninterested in anything other than itself; it has neither compassion nor empathy for others. A person who is strongly influenced by this force sows seeds of discord and discontent, and is arrogant, cold and ruthless toward others. Wealthy people start to feel more important than others do, or those who dress fashionably despise those who dress plainly. Some people are made aggressive once they acquire weapons that make them feel stronger.

The vegetable force is impacts on us in a different way. Material objects cannot move by themselves, but plants can grow once they are nourished. Plants have an insatiable appetite for growth, and people influenced by this force become hard workers. However, in terms of being considerate of others, they are not much different from those influenced by the material force. They are highly competitive and do everything to knock back others so that they themselves can come first. While always trying to be cleverer than anyone else, they are greedy and loath to let anyone overtake them, let alone be equal to them.

The animal force is also a source of energy for humans. Animals have a broad range of movement, have companions, and pursue the opposite sex. In order to survive this world, humans need to have sufficient passion and strength of will to overcome the many obstacles put in their way. The animal force helps to supplement that strength. However, this force can cause some to be seized by a desire to possess whatever they see or imagine, to be ruthless toward vulnerable people and be willing to commit cruel acts to get hold of their objective.

In contrast, the ordinary human life force allows us to lead a life that differs from that of animals. This life force enables us to control and moderate the desires that emerge from the three lower life forces below. People influenced by this force are calm, yield to others, and prefer harmony. They are able to remember their respect for God and their duties to humanity. This gives them the impetus to help others in strife. Thus, society is born, culture is fostered, and civilization develops. However, this force is not without its weaknesses. Basically, people may not be able to separate from self-interest and the egocentric behaviour that it fosters, and this tends to create problems for others who become caught up in that person's mistakes. If humans were capable of having a much wider, more accepting heart, we would be able to feel the unity of the human race on this earth.

The Higher Life Forces

The universe is comprised of these four forces as well as the three higher life forces. Bapak did not speak so much about these three higher worlds, as they are beyond our imagination. He only mentioned the names of these upper worlds as Rohani, which is the realm of the perfected, true human being; Rachmani, which is the realm of the mercy of God; and Rabbani, which is the realm that concerns the creation of God.

Human beings have a special relationship with the Rohani force, which is the third level from the top. As suggested by its name, meaning "perfect human being," the Rohani realm is the true home of the human soul and its destination after death. God intended the human soul to contain within it the Rohani life force. Adam was the first human to be created and he was also the soul of the Rohani realm. When Adam was in the Rohani world, he did not have a material body and was able to act freely and do as he wished. When a human physical body was fully created as a material being to exist on earth, Adam was sent down to our world to become the content of the human soul. As a result, he was limited to operating in this world solely through the physical functions he was endowed with. The reason for this, Bapak explained was that it was important for a Rohani soul to fully experience our earthly world and then return to the Rohani world with that experience and knowledge. This was also of benefit in other realms above human beings. He mentioned purposefully the words "human" and "human soul," because as humans, we are grounded by our material bodies but with souls that are filled with the ordinary human life force. The arrival of Adam on earth allowed the creation of true human beings whose souls contain the higher Rohani life force. At the same time, since we are still limited by our physical bodies, our soul can contain within it the material, vegetable, and animal life forces, which are below us.

The core powers of God exist above the seven levels of the universe. One of these is the Roh Ilofi, which Bapak called, the Great Life. This is God's power of creation and it flows through to the most profound depths of all seven realms. Another is the Roh Kudus, which extends over the universe from the outside. The Kudus are the angelic beings. The Great Life also acts as pathways connecting all seven worlds (like a stairway to Heaven). The soul that has improved itself in the lower world passes into the upper worlds through these pathways.

The above section is simply a summary of the basic framework of the cosmology Bapak spoke of, and therefore, may be difficult to understand. As I have said repeatedly, in no way does this represent a teaching or dogma of Subud.

The Home of the Human Soul

Bapak compared the human condition to that of a person building a house. The building of a house requires not just architects, but drafters, site supervisors, carpenters, plasterers, plumbers, and construction workers. All of these workers have to cooperate with each on instructions from the architect. It is not the architect's job to plaster the wall, nor the construction worker's job to give instructions instead of the architect. No one can do the other's job and then bill the owner for the work. However, that is exactly what is happening inside people today. The life forces are competing with each other for authority, and the human soul, which should be supervising them, is sleeping instead. The lower life force that wins the battle is the one controlling the person and the one who appears to be the leader.

The latihan puts an end to this confused state of affairs where the tail is wagging the dog. This requires us to be aware of the existence and behavior of each of the lower life forces within us. And this, in turn, requires uncommonly pure and sensitive inner feelings. It is possible for us to sense the exquisitely fine power of the spiritual world and to understand how these forces work inside of us.

In *Susila Budhi Dharma*, Bapak describes this state of understanding as the final stages of our purification. This state is certainly possible, but for me, myself, is a lofty goal I'm not sure I can reach—even after a lifetime of effort. All I can say is that I am on the path. I have benefited greatly from Subud, but in terms of purification, I am still a long way off from achieving it.

36

My own experience helps me to be mindful. Even if I cannot feel the actual lower life forces within, I can quickly detect the movement of negative energy generated by them. These negative energies manifest as negative thoughts and emotions, and by picking up the signs soon and quietening them from a state of latihan, I am able to control them indirectly. Bapak called the state wherein one recognizes the life forces directly, the state of 'preparedness.' This refers to the state of being prepared to enter the world of Rohani as a complete human being.

Knowing that it's almost impossible to create an ideal society for human beings yet still trying to discover how much we are capable of, defines us as human beings. Our bodies are composed of the life forces below the human level and our souls have been given the higher life force that is above the human. The more tragic we are, the more sublime we can be.

Relationship with the Material Universe – the Emergence of Quantum Theory

Rapid developments in cosmic data measuring technologies have confirmed that our universe is more expansive than we ever imagined. The Milky Way galaxy, to which our sun belongs, contains more than 100 billion stars, planets and other astral bodies, while the entire universe contains over 100 billion other galaxies like the Milky Way. Yet, according to Bapak, if we compare sizes, this vast material universe would occupy only a small portion at the bottom of the infinitely larger spiritual universe.

Matter consists of a collection of particles that are rigid bodies. At any point in time, matter occupies a designated location, and in principle, does not permit other matter to occupy the same space. We build fences around our homes and lock doors to keep thieves out. Matter behaves in the same way. On the other hand, a vibration does not occupy a specific location at a specific point in time, but exists everywhere in space, within a given range of probability.

Matter and vibrations exist separately and have different properties. Conventional logic in physics says that it is not possible for an object to share both properties simultaneously. People believed that something that could not be observed, felt, or measured could not exist. Research into elementary particles and the emergence of quantum physics (quantum theory) has reversed that logic. The properties and behavior of elementary particles— the newly discovered smallest unit of matter—are extraordinary. They are beyond the laws of physics – and even common sense. It is impossible for humans to observe the elementary particles of waves. When we try to measure waves, they strangely disappear and transform into rigid bodies (particles). In fact, elementary particles are both particles and waves at the same time. The discovery of quantum theory created a massive paradigm shift in our thinking. This paradigm shift is on a bigger scale than the transition from the Ptolemaic theory to the Copernican theory in the Middle Ages. When Copernicus' proposal that the earth orbits the sun was proved to be true, it triggered the Renaissance and a transition from the religion-dominated world, to a modern society. Quantum theory may create an even more radical paradigm shift than this. However, it will be probably be closer to fifty or even one hundred years before we fully understand the implications of this.

Quantum theory is challenging to understand. The following section presents my limited understanding of the infinitely strange world of elementary particles. The experience of this peculiarity and wonder might even be close to the latihan itself. Bapak's explanations are not contradicted by any of these theories.

The Impact of Quantum Theory

Most people have been taught in school that the smallest physical unit is the atom and elements are made up of clusters of them. Since atoms are particles (solid, rigid bodies), the material universe which is a collection of these, is the only reality that exists.

Major innovations in instruments of observation from the end of the 19th century over the 20th century, revealed that atoms were made up of even finer particles and classical physics was no longer applicable. This was the birth of quantum theory and quantum mechanics. Then came the astonishing discovery that while electrons and photons, which are elementary particles, have the properties of particles, they also, simultaneously, have the incompatible properties of waves.

Particles are solid bodies that occupy a certain space at a certain point in time. If another solid body tries to enter that space at the same time, they will collide. Waves, on the other hand, expand outwards and can exist in more than one specific location at any given point in time so that they fill all the space available within a certain range of probability. It seems impossible that these particles can possess both solid and wave-like properties at the same time, but this is the reality of the world of elementary particles, the smallest units of matter. Here, common sense simply doesn't apply. That is probably why experts are using quantum theory to try to explain telepathy and other parapsychology phenomena but this research is still in its infancy.

Quantum particles have another interesting property. Some pairs of quanta have a mysterious relationship with each other called quantum fluctuation. These particles can relay their state to each other instantaneously, regardless of where they are in the universe. Terrestrial time is irrelevant. One particle could be on earth while the other particle could be at another corner of the universe hundreds and thousands of light years away—and yet that information is transmitted instantly.

Furthermore, elementary particles exhibit extraordinary behaviour in that they manifest as waves when no one is looking but manifest as solid entities when someone tries to observe them. This is one of the riddles of human observation, which, incomprehensibly, is in direct contradiction to our post-Descartes dualistic separation of mind and matter. What is unimaginable to us occurs continuously in the world of elementary particles.

For better or worse, events that occur in the micro quantum world do not interfere with events that occur in our everyday macro world and vice versa. This means we can go about our normal business without having to pay attention to elementary particles. However, elementary particles are the foundation of matter and no one can be certain that events that occur in the micro world have zero impact on the macro world.

Astonishing discoveries in the field of astronomy also proved that matter is not the predominant content of the universe, as was traditionally taught by science. The expansion of our universe is actually accelerating and this expansion is due to the existence of an unknown substance and energy in the universe, called dark matter and dark energy, respectively.

According to NASA, the ratio of these substances is as below:

- The ratio of matter to the entire universe is less than 5%
- Dark matter constitutes 27%
- Dark energy constitutes 68%

Until now, the universe was considered to be a conglomerate of atoms; therefore, 'matter' here means the total mass of atoms that exist in the universe. Dark matter is a very strange phenomenon in that it appears to have gravity in the same way that matter does, yet light cannot penetrate it or be reflected by it. We have hardly any understanding of dark energy; it exerts greater influence on the universe than all matter, yet it is an unknown form of energy that is not measurable, observable, nor made up of particles.

The fact that there are forces and energies present in the universe apart from matter (atoms) is astonishing. Even though it is an established fact, we find it hard to believe that matter, which until now was thought to be the entire mass of the universe, occupies a mere 5% of the universe and that the remaining 95% is made up of the completely unknown forces of dark matter and dark energy.

Personally, quantum theory and these new astronomical discoveries are the closest anything has come to how Bapak's saw the universe. He described the latihan as 'strange but real.' Coincidentally, Katsuhiko Sato, a world leader in space research and the theory of cosmic inflation, described the mystery of quantum theory as '...strange but apparently true, true but infinitely strange.' (*Author's quote*)

PART II

Explanations of the Opening and Latihan

1

THE WAITING PERIOD AND THE OPENING

Three-month Waiting Period

Anyone, regardless of their nationality, language, religion, or culture, can join Subud and start practicing the latihan. The latihan is a form of spiritual training that is for people who have a sincere desire to change themselves. Joining out of an idle wish just to try it out will result in few benefits. That is why there is a waiting period of three months before joining. During that time, the applicant has several meetings with Subud members designated as "helpers" (people who have been in Subud a long time who are responsible for the opening of new members). At these meetings, they can ask any questions they may have to help to deepen their understanding.

The latihan of Subud is based on a new awareness of thoughts and emotions that has no precedent. Therefore, applicants need to know in advance, what they can and cannot expect, and only then make a judgement as to whether the training is in line with what they had hoped for. This is to ensure there is no misunderstanding from the start and therefore no subsequent disappointment.

The initial application is provisional, and after the three months waiting period, the applicant can then state whether they still wish to join. New applicants need to be 17 years of age or over—the age which society agrees is when people can make their own decisions about how to act based on their own judgement. The following are topics that are discussed during the waiting period.

In latihan, we don't need to do anything; indeed, it is *important* that we do nothing. All we need to do is trust in the unknown force that works in the latihan, to accept its promptings and to give ourselves up to it unconditionally. Complete surrender is the foundation of Subud, but not many people truly understand what this signifies. Applicants need to talk over the nature of and need for this surrender with the Subud helpers they have been meeting with during their application period so they can understand the principles of Subud and agree to them.

Applicants can practice the latihan once they have been opened. The opening occurs when they do their first latihan accompanied by the helpers. Before they are opened, applicants are asked to make a short statement of commitment. These words state, "I believe in the One Almighty God and I wish to worship only Him." The use of the word "God" may be an issue for people who do not believe in the existence of God. The statement can be reworded to reflect the beliefs of the person, such as, "If God does exist, then I wish to believe in Him," or, "Should an unknown force manifest within me, I will follow this movement," or words to that effect. Regardless of how it is worded, the latihan remains a training whereby a person accepts the workings of an unknown force, which they feel inside themselves and whose promptings they follow. The statement of commitment is an act confirming a person's ultimate consent to undertake the training. In Subud, where experience is everything, those who can say they believe in

God do so because they have had experiences that have convinced them of this belief. Any belief – or even disbelief – that is not based on personal experience is like a veil that obscures spiritual truth. When we make a commitment and are opened, the veil needs to be lifted, even if only by a miniscule amount. In Subud, there is no requirement for people to have belief–unless they experience it for themselves. This is one of the characteristics of Subud, which also demonstrates the fact that it is not a religion or teaching.

Discussions during this waiting period will no doubt turn to illness and the latihan. While many members have experienced the beneficial effects of the latihan on their health, it is against the principles of Subud to practice latihan with the aim of curing illnesses. Trusting in God means transcending the issue of being cured or not, instead submitting oneself to God and following God's will. In the early days of Subud, a Hungarian actress who had uterine cancer and became pregnant made headlines when her cancer was cured after she started practicing the latihan and she was able to have the baby. It is important to state that curing illness is not an objective of the latihan. When members become ill, the helpers may visit that person at home and do a special latihan with them; but this does not happen with the aim of curing their illness. The purpose of doing latihan together is to help that member to deepen their surrender to God. If subsequently their illness is cured, this is thanks to the will and the grace of God, and not due to their latihan.

On the other hand, it also happens that through the process of purification, a person's condition worsens and, for a short time, they show symptoms similar to those of an illness. In some cases, if the member had an underlying condition, this can come to the surface. Again, this is not the direct result of practicing the latihan, but the process of purification may have hastened the surfacing of that condition. If the condition manifests with the physical symptoms of a disease, the best thing to do is to consult a doctor or medical expert.

One of the rare things that can occur in connection with the latihan is a state of 'crisis,' when a member may experience a temporary mental or physical imbalance and be unable to live life normally. This is more likely to occur if someone is impatient to make progress and keeps increasing the number of latihans they do, which in turn induces changes that they are unable to withstand. Crises do not usually last longer than three months, but they may disrupt family life and confuse people around the person, as they often manifest as a mental illness. In the case of a crisis, helpers need to take care of the person while maintaining their own inner calm. To prevent a crisis from happening in the first place, it is important to keep to the prescribed latihan times and to leave the speed of one's progress in God's hands.

There are, in fact, different types of crises. Some members may have a spiritual imbalance and could be given stronger latihans to correct it so that they enter into a crisis-like state temporarily. This state is different from the kind of crisis that people who are eager for progress fall into when they do too many latihans. In the former case, a person may behave abnormally, but they do not cause confusion to the people around them. It is probably more appropriate to call this state one of intense purification rather than a crisis. In this state, members may experience dramatic, internal changes and find a new direction in their lives. This usually does not last longer than three months.

The circumstances are different for applicants who have a history of or a latent mental illness. In this case, if they are opened and their mental illness surfaces because it is stimulated by their latihan and purification, this state may last for longer than three months, unlike that of a crisis. In principle, the latihan of Subud is a form of training whereby one is changed and purified while living a normal life just like everyone else. Should an illness or disability prevent someone from carrying out life as normal, treatment for this condition takes precedence. In the case of a mental illness, it is a priority that the person gets treatment. Unfortunately, Subud does not yet have sufficient facilities or professional mental health staff that can care for such cases. As a precautionary measure, people with a mental illness are asked to wait until they are treated before being opened. If someone is opened with a latent mental illness that manifests later, the person still needs to seek treatment as a priority and is often advised to stop doing the latihan. Stopping the latihan does not mean severing the connection with Subud or cutting off all contact with the Great Life Force. This is the magic of Subud beyond our understanding; once a person is opened, this event happens in a space-time continuum that transcends this world and can never be undone. Even when a person stops doing the latihan, while the pace may slow and the method change, they continue to progress. This principle also applies to people with development disorders or neuroses.

Some people expect that since Subud is a spiritual training, the latihan will give them paranormal powers. They need to learn that this is not the case. On the contrary, if they have physic powers now, they may lose them once they start practicing the latihan. People's capabilities, including paranormal powers, have nothing to do with their humanity or spirituality. Subud acknowledges miracles wrought by God's power, but there is as much difference between these miracles and paranormal phenomena produced by human physic powers as there is between heaven and earth.

Paranormal powers and supernatural phenomena are mostly manifested on earth through the life forces that are below humans. Bapak mentioned that telepathy, which is an example of a supernatural power, uses the material force related to thinking. People who acquire abilities that others may not possess tend to feel superior and become obsessed with them. Once they join Subud, however, they often lose this power as it can hinder the progress of their souls. On the other hand, some people have an inherent sensitivity to the supernatural and they may have some form of clairvoyant or paranormal experiences. Such people are in the minority and it is possible that their inner feelings are already working a little but are mainly dormant due to some disturbance in their thoughts and emotions. As their inner feelings start to recover through the latihan, these experiences may disappear altogether or conversely, they may increase.

The three-month waiting period does not apply to people over sixty-five, people with a severe illness, and spouses of Subud members. If only one person in a couple wants to be opened, Subud advises them to discuss this with their partner and if possible, get their agreement before completing an application form. This is because the purification process initiated by the latihan affects everyone differently. Welcome or unwelcome changes that occur in someone can disturb their partner to the extent that they lay the blame solely on Subud.

What Happens at the Opening?

Once the three-month waiting period is over, and if the applicant still wishes to be opened, the date for the opening is decided.

At the opening, the person conducting the opening and other helpers do the latihan together with the applicant. There is no specific preparation before the opening. The helper conducting the opening gives the applicant some instructions about how to be during the process. This includes telling the applicant to shut their eyes, relax, and stand naturally; not to cross their arms, or clench their fists, or pay attention to any noises or sounds that the helpers around may make but only to allow themselves to feel their inner self. They are told not to try to force themselves to relax nor do they need to focus their mind but to completely trust the great power that works in the latihan and surrender themselves to the movements that arise from this. The opening begins when the accompanying helpers each start their own latihan. All the helpers need to do is to follow their own latihan as usual.

Any direction of thoughts or energy from applicant or helpers will interfere with the opening. This might suggest that nothing can happen at the opening, but in most cases, applicants will feel that something is initiated inside themselves. What someone experiences at their opening can go far beyond the physical, and no one can predict what the applicant will actually feel or experience at that time. In most cases, the person talks about feeling a vibration that is like an electric current prompting movement in a certain part of their body. Alternatively, many people just feel a physical urge to move. In fact, this vibration is not separate from the movement; the vibration is felt and the body moves. This movement can be felt in the hands, or the feet, the neck, the hips, or all. It is also possible that the applicant feels nothing during the opening—it depends strongly on their condition and their sensitivity. In some cases, it is simply a case of the applicant being too nervous to relax enough to feel anything. Even if this is the case, the applicant's opening has still been completed.

The helpers who accompany the opening simply do their own latihan, and therefore are not aware of what the applicant experiences; however, from the content of their own latihan they can sense the progress of the opening. The opening is the moment when the applicant's sleeping soul, shut inside their innermost self, encounters the Great Life that permeates the entire universe and wakes up, allowing that power to start to flow inside them. In his book, *Susila Budhi Dharma*, Bapak described it as follows:

"...soon after the mind has stopped thinking and has been separated from the feelings as a result of the opening, a vibration of life is felt, which goes on to encompass the whole body and soon causes movements that seem very strange to the mind.

This state is indeed truly strange to the mind, because it is not something that the thought can bring into being but something real that can be received and witnessed by a feeling no longer influenced by thinking.

Once you have received and witnessed this reality, you will start to truly feel what is happening inside you. By so doing, you will get an indication of the right path: moreover, the authenticity of the true self will become apparent.

Because of this, you will see what faults you have always borne—faults caused by your parents' conduct before their child came into existence.

This state is something truly remarkable, because in the degree to which one can attain it, it reveals the qualities a person lacks for his status as a human being, the lack of which makes his chance of reaching higher levels, or the realm of perfection, very slight."[5]

However, I personally have never witnessed anyone experiencing everything Bapak described in this quote. This is probably because in our times, human beings are polluted internally by the accumulation of dirt and defects, and have almost completely lost any spiritual sensitivity. At their opening, most people feel prompted to move by an unfamiliar force, or, at best, a bodily vibration. What Bapak mentions as an outcome of the opening should be viewed as a reference to the spiritual truths that members may experience someday through their subsequent Subud life and purification.

If the helpers doing latihan with the applicant at the opening feel nothing and it is unclear whether that person has been opened or not, after some time, or even days, that person can be opened again. The person should not feel discouraged if this is the case. The awakened soul, if cared for properly afterwards, will put forth shoots at some stage. Proper care means continuing to take part in group latihans even if the person feels nothing. Once that person can do latihan by themselves, the delay in their start will have no impact on their later progress. Patience is necessary. The exercise of patience will be a big asset to that person later on.

Subud understands the weakness of human beings and completely respects members' decisions, which are made from their free will. If a member wishes to leave, he/she is not prevented from doing so.

The Spiritual Process of the Opening

The opening occurs in a spiritual place that appears inside us. It emerges in our innermost self through the effect of the latihan. A person's opening is effective while they are carrying out their latihan, but this also has effect in the world after death. Bapak did not speak about this in detail, but he did caution members not to take their opening lightly.

The way Bapak explained it was that the Great Life is a creative force that penetrates the entire universe. At the moment of the opening, it passes through everything and everyone present and brings them together as one. If the applicant is able to have an attitude of complete surrender to the Great Life, they too will be enveloped by its influence as it flows through the helpers doing the accompanying latihan. What happens is that a kind of inner path is created inside both applicant and helpers so that the Great Life flowing through the helpers can pass through to the inner self of the applicant. This is the first thing that needs to happen.

The next condition to help that new member to do their own latihan is that the faults that compressed their soul until now, blocking their contact with the Great Life, be partially removed, allowing their soul to wake up. The applicant cannot do this by himself or herself. The opener and accompanying helpers unwittingly fulfil that role in accordance with the will of God. In other words, they shoulder some of the burden that the new member was carrying. This cooperation between members is unique in that it does not come from our will or consciousness but through surrender. This is explained further by Bapak in Susila Budhi Dharma as below.

"...the person who is the link (the opener) probably deserves to be commended because at that moment, he will at least experience the unpleasantness of the suffering in feelings released from the body of the person being opened, while the latter, on the contrary, will feel as if relieved of a heavy burden.

54

So you must not be satisfied with just reaching that stage; rather, when standing (as a helper) by a brother who is being opened, do feel what is being received, so that you not only witness what is happening to him but can also receive what you need for your own self.

In this state, you can make good progress, for it will become apparent how the forces that have gathered in the feelings combine and separate.

By this means, the suffering that comes to you from helping or opening a new member will no longer be a heavy burden, but will even increase your own smooth progress toward the identity of a human being. Moreover, because you are in this state, the opening will be more satisfactory for the member you are standing by."[10]

Once someone has been opened, they can join in the group latihans that take place in their local group. As a rule, they do latihan twice a week, thirty minutes at a time. While new members can eventually do latihans by themselves, it is best to join in the group latihans. Most Subud members are aware that they receive more when they do their latihan in a group rather than when they do it alone. Perhaps this is because the same kind of mutual help mentioned above at the opening is operating in another realm at God's discretion.

SUBUD AND EVERYDAY LIFE

The Easy and the Difficult in Subud

Simply doing the latihan is easy. When we have the intention to do latihan and we turn our attention to God or to our inner selves, the latihan seems to start automatically. Once someone gets used to latihan, it can be done anywhere, anytime. The changes that are felt in the early stages of doing latihan differ from person to person; people may find they are drawn to a new type of food, or activity.

In my own case, I began to care less about trivial things that would have bothered me before. Probably many other people similarly became calmer than they had been before. I remember being asked three months after my opening if I was aware of any changes, and replying that I was. My dreams had started to change. I used to dream in black and white, whereas now I saw vivid colours. The dreams were about running from floods or big waves or animals, which I was sometimes frightened of or sometimes tamed. I was surprised that I would sometimes dream of ancient creatures from the age of dinosaurs. I gradually became aware that these dreams indicated the continuing purification of my feelings. I remember once being happy that in one of my dreams, I saw a shabby, little, grey bird transform into a vividly coloured phoenix and fly away before my eyes.

Some people have the opposite experience and become short-tempered after their opening. Their anger is chased out by the latihan and starts to surface. These are all signs of the transformation of self that occurs because of the latihan. We never know when this is going to happen. The changes are subtle and easily overlooked if we don't pay attention to them. So, one of the important rules in Subud is to pay close attention to changes and not ignore them. No one can tell us what will happen in our latihan or why because it comes from a force that transcends our world.

Each person's latihan is different and unpredictable. One latihan might be a wonderful experience but there is absolutely no guarantee that the subsequent latihans will also be as wonderful. Oftentimes, the following latihans are simply "business as usual" and continue so for months. Anyone observing their own latihan over a lengthy period will see that the content unmistakably changes and continues to so; like the changes in a child as they grow up. Sometimes, members feel challenged because the changes seem to have slowed down and their progress halted. Their latihan feels stuck as though they are on a treadmill.

In such a case, members have a means to understand and resolve spiritual issues in the form of "testing" (explained below in "The Gift of Testing"). There are conditions to allow testing to take place in the right way and not all issues can be solved through testing. In these cases, the member needs to persevere with their latihan in its current state and wait until it can change. It can be challenging for some people to trust in Subud and continue with their stubbornly unchanging latihan, not knowing why or how long it will last.

So that our effort and patience could be strengthened, Bapak gave members possible reasons as to why someone's latihan may not change. The state of our latihan reflects the state of our purification at that time. When we continue to have the same latihan repeatedly for a lengthy period, it is because we are being purified of a stubborn layer of dirt that is as hard as a rock. To borrow a medical metaphor, purification in the latihan is like a non-invasive treatment that does not harm healthy organs or tissue or cause pain or suffering in the way that invasive surgery does. The same process needs to be repeated again and again depending on the extent or type of the issue (dirt). For example, the issue may be an intrinsic personality trait you inherited from your parents or ancestors. It is very challenging to remove this type of fault unless the person becomes aware of it and is serious about trying to eradicate it. As I mentioned in the earlier section about purification, unless people recognize this themselves, their latihan will stay the same indefinitely. This is one of the challenges of the latihan. You might feel that even though you are working hard in your latihan, you just cannot move forward from where you are at that moment. However, members who have this type of latihan will find that at some point, they too will be able to progress to the next stage.

We live in difficult times. Society is changing rapidly and everyone wants more speed and efficiency in his or her life. The desire for instant gratification is the norm, and there is no place for patience. Patience is rapidly being degraded as unnecessary and people are under intense pressure from a materialist society in flux. To resist this pressure, we need to trust in Subud and remain strong of heart.

The Meaning of Progress in the Latihan

How do you know if your latihan has progressed or not? We don't have a lot of self-knowledge and consequently tend to look outward rather than inward. Our thoughts and emotions are very helpful in our lives when it comes to analysing the world around us, but they are less capable when it comes to recognizing what is inside of us. It is no wonder then, that we are very good at seeing the faults in others and not so good at seeing our own.

We often rely on professionals to change our behaviour, and then we exercise our will to overcome our weaknesses. Complete success is rarely the result. This is because the will, which initiates the effort, has weaknesses within itself that become mixed up with the original issues. Ironically, using the will to correct one's faults can actually result in strengthening them in a different direction. Furthermore, people who point out our faults only see the obvious ones. Therefore, we end up correcting only those while our heart and mind that created them stay the same.

The training that occurs in Subud uses a power completely separate from our will or effort where we are reformed through purification by the Great Life. This correction will not occur unless the person recognizes and accepts their own weaknesses. In principle, the Great Life does not force changes on anyone against their free will. That is why Subud places so much importance on becoming aware of your own weaknesses.

Purification through the latihan begins with the external faculties of the body and the five senses. As it progresses to the more complex inner functions of the thoughts and feelings, the challenges increase.

Latihan in Everyday Life

New members are told at the start, that apart from doing the latihan twice a week, they don't need to change anything in their day-to-day lives. Their process of purification will result in changes after they have been doing the latihan for some time. At that stage, not accepting these changes may actually hinder the progress of their purification. Bapak explained this situation using the example of an ashtray. Even if you clean out an ashtray that is full of cigarette butts, if you can't quit smoking, the ashtray will soon be full again. If this situation continues to be repeated, the ashtray will never become clean. One step forward becomes one step back in an endless loop. Subud members who have undergone purification need to pay attention that they don't carry back inside themselves the dirt they have just rinsed away; to continue the metaphor, they need to either resist or give up smoking altogether.

While the latihan itself needs no help from humans, effort is required not to block the appropriate purification process. This doesn't mean 'doing' something so much as 'not doing' certain actions the person has continued habitually until now. Once a member starts doing latihan, they become calmer and less bothered by trivial things, showing that purification has begun. Suppose that member then receives an intense shock that disturbs their feelings and they can't suppress their agitation. This means that the purification has not yet reached their innermost feelings. Normally, that person can do nothing about this. They can dissipate this energy as anger or simply wait until this agitation subsides naturally, however long it takes. Most people have weakened inner feelings and have no means or power to control their emotions. Even people in Subud will not be able to progress with their purification unless they bring about changes. Every time they become irritated, the energy of their anger and agitation is reproduced and leaves a residue. That is where members need to use the latihan that is already within them. It doesn't show itself normally and may appear not to exist at all, yet it is still there inside and has not been lost. A member can call upon the latihan at any time and find it inside them.

Subud members can use this to control the workings of their emotions in everyday life. Of course, this is not about visibly doing the latihan in your workplace or in public, but rather about being in a latihan-like state where possible and allowing yourself to feel the calmness and quietness that this brings about. This is about putting to use what we receive in latihan in our everyday lives, as Bapak encouraged. We need to remember that the latihan exists within us and we can reproduce inside ourselves the inner calm and peace that we feel when the Great Life is at work. Varindra Vittachi, a member I knew well, once uniquely described it as, 'the feeling of butterflies beating their wings inside my chest and about to take flight.' Even though a person may not be in full latihan, their feelings will quieten and become calm, and a few seconds later, their normal state will return without anyone noticing. Should you do this several times throughout your day, you will find that before you start to feel irritated or angry, your mind becomes less agitated and your feelings calm.

If you continue to do this, you will gradually understand your true inner state when it is not under the influence of your thoughts and emotions. By knowing the difference between the two states, you should be more sensitive to these signs before your emotions start to run wild. Once they have run off, like wild horses, they are hard to rein in. Being able to detect the signs makes it easier to calm down before the emotions get out of hand, and putting this into practice will transform the way your emotions operate in your daily life.

The movements and expressions that people make during latihan indicate the content of that person's inner feelings at that time. Your true self, or part of your true self, is shown in a way that is normally not available to you. If you are always keenly aware of your latihan and look back over your daily actions, you can come to know the state of your own inner feelings at that time. This gives you a means of gauging how much purification you still need to achieve an ideal human state. Humans have spent eons, since prehistoric times, in the continual pursuit of the desires required to live in this world. As a result, they have sacrificed the function of their inner feelings and degraded their original selves. Perhaps, these means were the only way left for God to show us how to regenerate ourselves spiritually. It is possible that because this is how things were, God chose not to send the latihan of Subud to this world through the teachings and warnings of a prophet. I believe Bapak understood that God provided this extraordinary method in order to manifest the Great Life directly in this world in a way that was equivalent to God actually coming down into the world.

Once someone has experienced the latihan, their inner feelings, which were once dried up like a stone, are then given the moisture and nutrients they require by the human soul and gradually start to have their innate functions restored. Again, for this to happen, we need to have the patience and complete surrender that are the basis of Subud. Here, surrender means to believe that we are led by the power of the Great Life and to continue our latihan without doubting this. Patience means the ability to face reality and not give in to the desires of the heart.

Preparation for the Final Stage

This brings us to the question; where does this latihan practice lead to and what is the final stage. This stage is when one can live one's life always in a latihan state; when with progressive purification, the thoughts and emotions are transformed and no longer block the inflow of the Great Life. Contact with the Great Life is constantly maintained, even if thoughts and emotions fulfil their usual roles in everyday life; indeed, these become as servants, carrying out the commands of the soul.

A long time ago, Subud members could look to Bapak as a living example of this. Bapak was always in latihan. Whether he was talking to someone, drinking tea, or working, he was never separate from the latihan. I still vividly remember how Bapak showed through testing and his humorous demonstrations how even in the middle of accounting tasks; he was continually praising God, saying 'Allah! Allah!' inside himself. This is Subud's ultimate goal. If we could be in a state close to this, without doing anything, we would feel as though we were one with the latihan. No doubt, we would also use the thoughts and emotions that we need to exist in the world in a different way—we would make full use of them instead of them making full use of us. We would appreciate the cooperation of the life forces that are below the human force, while supervising their actions with our soul in command. We would constantly feel the presence of God close to us and realize that God is watching over us, protecting us, and guiding us.

None of this makes Subud members different from anyone else. Members experience the same difficulties as other people; have the same joys and sufferings, and the same illnesses. However, people who have acquired internal strength with the latihan can find a way through to the future without unduly disturbing their hearts and minds, no matter what they come up against. The latihan has been in the world for over sixty years. Only Bapak was able to experience fully the spiritual journey opened up by the latihan, but his experience showed us the potential of Subud.

Bapak said that the latihan is a special gift and grace from God, beyond human comprehension. If we use our heart and mind to try to understand the latihan, we will only end up by impeding any real progress. He did not refer to a specific example of this, but as I understand it, a typical case might be of a member who lacks confidence and trust in their own latihan, instead tries to find authority and reliance in Bapak's words instead. They often attach great importance to Bapak's words as well as their own interpretation of Bapak's words, obstinately quoting these in every situation, and mistakenly believing that this is the proof of a good Subud member.

It is true that the content of our own latihan is still unreliable in many cases, and this is the reason why we still need to refer to Bapak's explanations and advice. However, the latihan is a way to improve ourselves, as we follow the guidance of the Great Life. Purification proceeds day by day through the working of the latihan, and this process brings about a radical change in ourselves. Bapak did not intend that we should place his words above the meaning of the latihan itself. To do so is would create a fundamental approach to Subud that attempts to transform the latihan into a religion.

The significance of the latihan experience is that it opens up a new way for people to experience spiritual truth for themselves. While this may be fragmentary in the beginning, as we continue the latihan, we are able to witness the reality of the spiritual world.

This allows us to recognize the gap between our understanding and the reality and to make our own decisions about how we want to live our lives. That is the significance and purpose of the latihan of Subud as guided by the Great Life.

The latihan brings enormous blessings. The creative force of the Great Life changes people from their very foundations and gives them the potential to have their human souls lifted up. Even if a person is not completely purified, they receive many benefits in their process towards purification. Once a person is purified, they can start to feel the four lower life forces that make up the human body and inform their actions. These life forces are very fine spiritual energies, so it requires much sensitivity and very pure inner feelings to sense them. Once you can be aware of and identify each life force, you can then direct and guide all the lower forces, enabling them to carry out their proper role as your assistants. That is the purpose of purification. In this case, you can also fully repay these lower forces for their services to you because if it is God's will, we can help them return to their true homes after we die. Bapak called this work preparation for life after purification. This refers to the preparation to be raised, with the help of God's power, from the fourth level of this ordinary human world to the realm of the Rohani that is above the human level. If we can approach that state, our life in this world will be mightily transformed.

It is hard to explain and to understand how events that occur in the spiritual realm can manifest in this material world; in the spiritual world, positions are switched around. For example, money is the symbol of wealth. Normally, people chase after money so they can keep it. In this case, money is of a higher status than people are. In other words, money is positioned to control people. It is the reverse for people who have positioned their human soul at the centre of their being. They do not chase money, but rather money follows them, longing for them to be their master. Such a person will never be hard up for money from that moment onwards—though not of course, if they want to have more money than they need. They will find it easier to make enough money for living and, in addition, that money comes to them in unexpected ways. This is the same with other situations; once their human souls have taken up position inside themselves, people will intrinsically behave more like humans and this will flow out to their surroundings.

3

THE DIFFERENT STAGES OF THE LATIHAN

Bapak's Guidance

Between 1957 and 1987, Bapak travelled the equivalent of about twenty-four laps of the earth. He gave talks to members around the world, explaining the meaning and principles of the latihan. These talks, numbering over 1,300, were translated—and are still being translated into English and several other languages.

As I described earlier, Bapak received the latihan in an extraordinary manner and experienced its potential through intense training. He was without doubt the most appropriate person to bring Subud to the world. Yet, he never once gave a talk to the public, instead only ever addressed Subud members. He also advised members not to try to understand his talks with their minds, but to only listen and feel whatever could be felt at that time. Actually, for anyone practicing the latihan, the right way to listen or read Bapak's talks is probably in a state that is close to a latihan state.

Reportedly, when Bapak was asked why he did not give his talks to the public, he replied that it was up to members to explain Subud to people in their own countries, using the language and words that were familiar to them. There is no universal language for all of humankind, and languages around the world reflect the characteristics of each culture.

Bapak was Indonesian and he was brought up in the culture of Islam. Naturally, his talks contain many Islamic words and expressions. If he were born in a Christian country, his words would reflect Christianity. Behind Bapak's encouragement to members to explain Subud in their own languages is also the conviction that Subud is not just for a prescribed culture or religion, but also for the benefit of the whole of humankind.

Bapak said repeatedly in his talks that Subud was not a religion or a teaching but an experience. While they are a precious source of understanding for most Subud members, he did not make his talks open to the public so as not to invite misunderstanding. This book is largely based on Bapak's talks. Reading his talks on a superficial level could lead to the misconception that they are teachings after all.

Throughout his life, Bapak never allowed himself to be called a teacher or a leader, but insisted his role was that of a spiritual guide - one who could show the way to the border of the spiritual world. This journey was made possible through the new experience of the latihan. His role was like that of a Sherpa for mountain climbers or a navigator in unknown waters. Indeed, Bapak's talks are like rough sketches or roadmaps for a journey never before taken. They are filled with information and guidance in the form of stories that act like landmarks on a long journey or signposts when the road forks. To see these talks as teachings or theories is a mistake, nor should they be received unconditionally as doctrine.

The entire process of the Subud journey is not a short one that you pack an overnight suitcase for, because the destination is a realm beyond the borders of the human world. It is my own opinion that while the Nirvana of the Buddhists might differ in name, spiritually speaking, it is the same thing. According to Buddhist teachings, for an ordinary human being to reach Nirvana, they must be reincarnated many times, and this can take an infinity. Bapak mentioned that the latihan of Subud greatly shortens this process. Instead of having to be reincarnated multiple times, we have the possibility of ascending directly to heaven. This begs the question, why were we given the latihan of Subud? It also relates to the bigger question of what are human beings and what is their purpose.

We don't have the answers to those questions. No one does. The real question here is not people's individual understanding but the fundamental meaning of human existence and our relationship with all of nature and the cosmos. You won't get answers from the earthworm or the mole if you ask them the reason for their existence. To understand their lives and behaviour, you have to look to their relationship with nature. They collaborate with nature and their actions improve the soil, which in turn, supports the lives of plants and other small animals.

Most people think that the apex of human knowledge is science, but even scientists cannot tell us the meaning of our existence. Science provides answers as to how matter came about, but it is not the role of science to explore the mystery at the core of creation, namely, *why* it was created in the first place.

The Never-Ending Questions of Humanity
Chapter 4 of Part I described the seven life forces and the cosmology, which was Bapak's answer in relation to this fundamental question of the purpose of our existence. No one

can prove that what Bapak says is the truth. Bapak said that he did not talk about anything that he had not directly experienced himself. While he did not describe his full experience of the cosmology of the universe, he explained this graphically through his creation of the Subud symbol.

The symbol that Bapak chose to represent Subud consists of seven concentric circles, intersected by seven radiating lines. Bapak mentioned that it was better to imagine this as a three-dimensional, layered sphere rather than as a two-dimensional circle. The smallest area in the middle represents the material world. This is enveloped by the worlds of the lower forces in turn, in six wider circles fanning out from the centre. The seven diagonal radiating lines intersect with all seven layers and represent the Great Life force. This seven-layered universe is enveloped by and filled with the Roh Ilofi and the Roh Kudus, the direct power of God.

The idea that human beings are not material bodies but are souls with a higher spiritual existence has been around a long time and is not something thought up by Bapak. The Old Testament describes how God created humans out of soil and then breathed the life of the spirit into them. Gnosticism claimed that this world was not created by a good God, but by an evil angel who opposed God and that the human soul fell to earth from heaven and is trapped in this fallen world. This is similar to the Buddhist belief that we live in a world of suffering. Nevertheless, Bapak's ideas were not a reworking of Gnosticism. Some people also suggest that Bapak's cosmology was heavily influenced by the mysticism indigenous to the island of Java in Indonesia where he was born. Bapak respected religion, believing that while religions may include mistaken beliefs or misdirection, they do communicate many truths to people. He recommended Subud members to hold on to their own religions. The religious traditions of the past talked about true cosmic consciousness. Bapak was also able to experience this for himself and, no doubt, it is this same concept of awareness that he shared.

The Meaning of Complete Surrender

I have already stressed that total surrender to God is required for us to receive the latihan. This is the basis of Subud, and at this point, I would like to elaborate more on what this means.

A classic example of total surrender to God is that of Abraham as written in the Old Testament of the Bible. "And God wanted to test Abraham, so He said to him, 'Abraham!' to which Abraham replied, 'I am here!' And God said, 'Take your beloved son Isaac to the land of Moriah and sacrifice him on the hill that I shall designate!' [Genesis 22: 1-3 NrLV][6]" In other words, Abraham was asked to kill his son Isaac who was born to him in his old age and offer him up as a sacrifice to God. Even in the face of this command, which anyone might view as unreasonable, Abraham did not utter one word of protest but prepared himself to carry it out. However, just as he was about to lower the knife, God intervened and told him to kill a ram God had prepared instead of his son.

Many people reading this story may think this was a cruel command from God. Nevertheless, we must pay attention to the words, "…in order to test Abraham." God knew that Abraham was His loyal servant and He tested (trained) Abraham in this way in order to prove this in real terms in the real world. To Abraham, his son was everything—the thing that was more important to him than his life. This total surrender to God that Abraham showed is not something that we are capable of even if we desired it. If his surrender was one hundred percent, we can manage no more than ten percent or at the most, thirty percent. Since the amount of contact with the Great Life that we receive is proportionate to the size of the space within us that we have created within ourselves through our surrender, the benefits we can receive from our latihan can only be in proportion with this, too.

If a person's capacity to surrender is twenty percent say, then the inner space that person has opened up to receive the Great Life is also twenty percent. That is not enough space to carry out the work of purification. In order for our purification to progress smoothly, we need to prepare a sufficiently wide space within ourselves. In order for us to do this, we need to clean out the impurities that have been sitting there. As Bapak explained it, the act of surrender is moving forward by letting go.

Because we live in the reality of this world, there is no guarantee that when a person verbally claims, "I will carry out God's will and surrender to God" they can or will actually carry out this claim. At their opening in Subud, the applicant makes a brief verbal commitment to do this. If this surrender is shallow, the contact with the Great Life will be shallow and purification will not progress. By doing the latihan with the correct attitude, a member can gradually deepen their own surrender and finally give content to their verbal commitment.

Of course, to surrender means to submit everything one holds and possesses to the will of God. This "everything" includes within it everything one loves, everything one cannot bear to part with, everything that has gradually become parts of ourselves. The "impurities" I mentioned earlier that inhabit our inner space, include the things we love the most; anything we feel attached to. These have been given to us by God, such as our own selves, our health, our future, our partners, parents and families, our assets, social status, popularity, and reputation. In addition are the things that do not belong to us; as we did not bring them with us when we were born, and we will not take them with us when we die. They are things that we have on temporary loan from God (or nature) to help us live in this world.

Not many people in contemporary society think like this. Most people cannot feel the existence of God. However, it is undeniable that these things do not actually "belong" to us. To allow the Great Life to enter us, we have to create space by letting go of our belief that we own these things. That is what Bapak means by 'going forward by letting go.' Our ability to receive the will of God and submit to it depends on our ability to happily surrender all, or part, of whatever we possess or whatever we cherish at that moment.

Complete surrender is not readily attainable. The reason why it was possible for Abraham was that he was already filled with the power of God and was already purified of distorted ideas, confused feelings, and other impediments to his surrender. Otherwise, even Abraham would have found it difficult to follow such an irrational order. Anyone on the Subud path should aim for Abraham's state of one hundred percent submission, remembering this is the ultimate goal for our surrender. We need to watch over our process of purification with patience, occasionally checking on the state of our own surrender so that we can increase its content In Subud, the utmost respect is paid to people's own free will, and the power that works in the latihan seems to adhere to the same principle. Your faults will never be washed away unless you, yourself, become aware of your own faults and have the desire to remove them.

Acceptance, Trust, Sincerity, Patience

Bapak explained that the correct attitude to receive the benefits of the latihan was to surrender but also to have acceptance, trust, obedience, sincerity and patience. Acceptance, trust, and obedience are intimately connected to complete surrender. This means having a wide heart that is open to what has been given by God through this world, even if it is not wished for, while trusting in the workings of the omniscient God. To have an attitude of sincerity is to steadily face reality and not try to run away from it no matter how challenging things might become. Patience is necessary in many aspects of Subud and it is an inner state, which allows you to confront any situation with a calm and undisturbed mind.

Human beings cannot know the nature of God or the will of God. This is because God—the creator of the universe exists on an astronomically different dimension to us, God's creations. One way to describe this difference between the creator and the created is to compare a human and a table made by a human. While the human maker of the table is familiar with the material the table is made of, its structure, design, and usage, the table itself knows nothing of this. It cannot even know that it is used by humans.

There should be a clear distinction between matters belonging to this world and matters belonging to the spiritual world. If members assume that once they practice the latihan, they don't have to use thoughts and emotions or make an effort in their worldly lives, they will be disappointed. The right way to be before God is to have an attitude of unconditional surrender to God's will. We need to maintain a close relationship with God through our practice of the latihan, and until God's design is manifested as the fruits of the latihan, to wait patiently with trust and an untroubled mind. Complete surrender is required for spiritual matters related to God, and progress in the latihan. On the other hand, to live and work in this world we need to make full use of and manage our thoughts and emotion, given to us by God for that purpose.

The Gift of Testing

People experience many things during their lifetime: boredom, alienation, happiness, sadness, challenges, excitement, and much more. Should they lose their way, Subud members have been given a precious form of help for all aspects of life. This is the testing process.

Testing is no different from latihan. In both processes, we believe in the Great Life that manifests itself in the latihan and subsequently entrust everything that may happen in the future to it. This does not change. The only difference is that with testing, we ask God about the issue at hand just before we start the latihan and then immediately enter a latihan state. During this time, we do not think of anything, least of all the nature of the issue, but leave everything in God's hands. And, strangely, the answer is given to us.

Testing is used when a question arises in our latihan, for example, when it seems like the content of someone's latihan keeps repeating itself, which suggests their progress has halted. In this case, the question to ask would be, 'Why does my latihan stay the same and what is it within me that is obstructing my progress?' Whether the person gets an answer or not depends on the will of God. In most cases, they are given some form of answer that will help them to make a decision.

People receive these answers in different ways. Some receive it through the physical movements of their head or face or limbs, while others will receive it as an inner feeling or as a visual image. Some express it verbally. It depends on where and how far the Great Life has penetrated within that person.

However, this is not to say that the answer they receive is always the correct one. The more significant the question for the asker, the more likely it is that it comes entangled with hopes and desires that hamper total surrender. That is why it is recommended that testing be carried out in the presence of helpers. The helpers have no desires or expectations around the question, and this allows the asker to deepen their surrender in the testing and to use the answers received by the helpers as a reference. It is by no means easy to try to forget the question and surrender completely to the testing. If you do not, there is a danger that the answer you receive does not come from God but from your own heart and is in line with your hopes and expectations.

At Subud gatherings, tests called "body tests" or "awareness tests" are often carried out. These tests are not about seeking solutions to separate questions or problems but rather for each member to discover how far their own latihan has progressed. It allows us to understand how deep and in which parts of our bodies the power of the latihan has penetrated. For example, questions asked at this test might include, "Where are your legs? What purpose are your legs for?" or, "Where are your hands? What purpose are your hands for?" Then, members can observe how their body responds to these questions in the latihan. If the power of the latihan has penetrated to a person's legs, then that person's legs may move involuntarily and start to walk, or may not move and simply twitch, for example. Body testing can be carried out for any body part, organ, or internal function. The member can then find out where the power of the latihan has penetrated them without having to ask others.

Testing is essentially a method for solving spiritual issues and questions that the heart and mind cannot answer. It is necessary to avoid using it as a way to solve worldly questions, which the mind and the heart can be used to solve. Like using a sashimi knife to cut a tree, testing like this will blunt the accuracy of the inner feelings. Testing is a gift to people who practice the latihan and is not the same as revelations or fortune telling. It should not be used out of curiosity. For example, testing to understand the state of angels may not give the desired answer but could also be an uncomfortable or even harmful experience. Only angels understand the state of angels. Unless God raises us to the level above humans, we cannot understand this higher world.

Testing can be used both for personal issues and to solve problems in the group. It is normal in Subud to include the results of testing as a reference when selecting committee chairpersons or other members.

Exploring Talent and the Self

Continuing with the theme of testing, an important issue that is of particular concern to young people is what direction to take in life and what talents they hold. Many people who have graduated from university still can't find their way. Our world is at a time of great change and the whole of society is being forcibly shaken. Traditional social foundations and value systems have been torn apart. Once accepted absolute certainties have disappeared, and all values have become relative. In this new world where there is no central core, young people feel an unfathomable anxiety about their future. They worry about their future and that of the world, and about their purpose or goals in life. In the absence of absolute standards, the trends towards personal development has grown enormously. What does Subud offer in the light of such needs?

Subud believes that we were each born with unique talents and if we use those talents to make a living, we will not only sense our purpose in life, but it will also encourage the development of our character and the growth of our soul. Subud members can test to discover their talent and even find work that suits this talent. This is not an easy task. While Bapak was still alive, many members relied on him to tell them what their talents were. Bapak had to spend many hours responding to the hundreds of letters he received every week with this request. After his death, Subud members relied on his eldest daughter, Ibu Rahayu, to take on this role. Now, that Ibu Rahayu is over ninety, she can no longer carry out this work and she advises members to try to discover their talents by themselves. She has said that to understand someone else's talent, one has to become one with that person's soul, and that is no easy task.

When my daughter was younger and had just graduated from university, she asked Bapak what her talent was when I was also present. On that occasion, members from Japan were queuing up to greet Bapak and shake his hand. When it was my daughter's turn, she greeted Bapak simply and immediately after, asked in English, "Bapak, what is my talent?" She knew that Bapak was able to understand some English, but I was a little taken aback.

Then Bapak replied in English, "It is that of a teacher." When she asked him which field this should be, he replied "English" and asked her if she liked English. Fortunately, she did! She had already studied in the UK, but not have teacher qualifications, and so, immediately afterwards, she went on to complete post-graduate studies and then got a job as a part-time English teacher at private universities—a job that she continues to this day. She loves her work as an English teacher and thanks God for her good fortune that Bapak identified her talent from such a young age.

This story also illustrates the importance of timing when it comes to choosing a career in line with one's talent. If you want to become a professional musician at the age of forty or fifty, unless you were a child virtuoso, it is virtually impossible to get an income from performing. To succeed in a career requires more than talent; several other conditions have to be fulfilled, which require time and money. Nevertheless, while talent testing has difficulties, regardless of your age, there is merit in discovering your own talents. Knowing your own character and leading a life that is in line with those talents makes it easier to have a sense of purpose and happiness in life.

In fact, if we continue to practice the latihan, our true character that lies hidden behind our personality—which is the face we put on for society—can start to reveal itself without having to test. The latihan is a training where, with the help of the Great Life, we recover our true selves. Whether we realise it or not, the superficial face of our personality is peeled away and our true selves begin to emerge. When this happens, it can also mean that the person has become stronger. They no longer worry so much about what people may think of them and are able to say what they truly believe. In this way, we come to have a more profound understanding of our original selves.

The World Beyond

I have touched on many different themes already, but I imagine the topic of most interest is where we go after we die. I mentioned that the latihan also has a great impact on life after death as well as on the tranquillity of our parents and ancestors. Nobody has died and come back to describe to us what happens in the life beyond, but there are many published works available based on information from psychics and mediums, or records of séances. Bapak often mentioned life after death in his talks, but he did not give general explanations to members about what happens to us after we die.

I do not know much about death, but I always believed in the existence of the afterlife and experiences I have had in my latihan have backed this up. I also thought that there was some truth to the claims of spiritualism and theosophy in this regard. Initially, I was sceptical of what Bapak said regarding life after death. My first experience of this was in 1961, when Bapak's talks were first translated. In the beginning, only four talks were allowed to be published, as until then, his talks were never made public. The first talk included the following explanation:

"As to the death by crucifixion: this symbolises that a perfect human being lives, as it were, between this world and the next. That is why tradition tells us that after he died, Jesus was the same as he was before he died. This shows that it is God's will that the human soul should be able to protect and pass on its individual understanding to all those who are still in coarse form. Thus Jesus, in his life after death, lost nothing that had become a part of his individuality. He could still see, hear, smell, speak and perceive; and everything that had been part of him was still there.[7]"

I was confused by Bapak's words. I was sure I had translated it correctly, but he seemed to be saying that until now, ordinary people could not see, hear, smell, or talk in life after death. That did not tally with my beliefs at the time.

We are made flesh to live in this world. We have five senses and various other intelligent functions so that we can see, hear, smell, taste and touch. I believed that when we die, we lose this body and are given a spiritual body in place of our physical one. Spiritualism is the belief that we are given dual bodies—the physical body and the spiritual body—that are connected to each other. After death, we abandon our physical body so that our spiritual body can start to function. In contrast, the theosophists believe in the theory of multiple bodies, which we have from birth, including the physical, etheric, astral, mental, and causal body. What shocked me about Bapak's words in this talk was a section that said if a child is born into this world with a limb missing or if he is paralysed in some way, this would be mirrored in the world beyond ours. This question stayed inside me for a long time, and it was many years before the shock subsided. Bapak's words contradicted both the claims of spiritualism and our ordinary understanding.

I mentioned previously that Bapak did not give general explanations about life after death to members. Only one person asked Bapak directly for his reasons for this. This was Varindra Tarzie Vittachi, who served for many years as the Subud World Association chair, and who was an internationally known journalist. After Bapak's death, Vittachi published *A Memoir of Subud* with the subtitle *Bouquets for Bapak*[8]. The book includes his interview with Bapak in which they talk about life after death. In response to Varindra's first question, which asked why Bapak did not give general explanations about life after death, Bapak responded: "You are not ready to receive and understand the full answer." He followed on to say, that he would only speak about it in broad terms, and that Varindra needed to emphasise this if he passed the content

81

on. Bapak was very clear that his words were to be taken as a general response so as not to be misconstrued. He then said there were three main destinations for the soul after death.

The most common of these is the one for people who during their lives in this world, recognized only material values and were preoccupied only with material things. The souls of such people after death are encrusted with material residue that is like an armour and they cannot exist outside of a material world. Like seeds, which cannot put forth shoots, they sink to the bottom of the material world.

The next most common destination is for people who have the feeling to honour God and are not as tainted by the material world as the first group. When they die, their souls hover above earth rather than inside it, yet they cannot escape the sphere of the material world. These souls manifest as ghosts and spirits sometimes visible to the living. One of the ways of avoiding this fate is to learn how to live a better life so that you can be reborn as a human being.

The last destination is the least common case; it is for people who as soon as they die, are raised up by God from the world of the ordinary human life force to the Rohani world, which is the realm of the complete human being.

To explain a little further, another difference between this world and the world after death is that in the latter you can't improve yourself by your own power. Unlike this world, which is made up of solid material, the world after death is made up of waves where matter cannot exist. Our souls, which are not material, continue to live in the world after death, while our material bodies remain behind in this world. The issue becomes what remains of the products of our hearts and minds which themselves are like vibrations. They do not have substance or shape like matter and so can travel to the other world along with the soul; however, there they cease to be active. This is because the physical body, which supplied energy to the heart and mind, ceases to exist and its activities stop at the moment prior to death. Bapak likened this to the heart and mind being locked up at death so that it is no longer possible to alter memories or the content of the heart and mind. As a result, it is not possible to lie to God or any other celestial being.

Humans improve themselves through the efforts of their hearts and minds, but as mentioned above, these functions are no longer available after death. In fact, there is another, more significant reason why improvement after death is difficult: it is because we need to acquire a spiritual body, which replaces the physical body we had on earth. The world after death is composed of waves; hence, we need a spiritual body also composed of waves. This spiritual body sees, hears touches, considers, and feels whatever is or happens in the world after death.

I was also puzzled by something that Bapak had said in a talk in relation to the state of Jesus after his resurrection. It was already my understanding that we needed a spiritual body in the world after death. Until then, my thinking had been rather noncommittal, either going with the theosophists and the theory of multiple spiritual bodies, or with the spiritualists and the dual spiritual and physical bodies, the former replacing the latter at death. However, Bapak stated that we aren't given a spiritual body automatically when we die; instead, we have to work for it. This understanding of reality that came through Subud is perhaps a first for humankind.

We are naturally given a material body in the wombs of our mothers so that we can start to live in this world. This is not the case for our spiritual body. It seems that while we are alive on earth, we can acquire one for ourselves through our good behaviour. Bapak also mentioned that we could attain this spiritual body through the latihan. When we practice the latihan, the Great Life that flows into us penetrates all parts and organs of our body. This means that not only do these parts of our physical body come back to life, our human soul, which until then, did not have a specific form, starts to take shape in line with these parts. In this way, for example, we receive our spiritual fingers, which will be needed by our spiritual body, then our spiritual hands, then our spiritual feet and so on, until gradually we are able to acquire a spiritual body in complete form.

That is all I will say about the world after death, based on Bapak's words on this matter. We should also be mindful of his reply that people are not yet ready to face the realities of death. He prefaced these explanations with the caution that they were provisional and that people's circumstances could always change.

4

INTERNATIONAL HARMONY AND SOCIAL CONTRIBUTION

International Harmony amongst Members

Subud members come from all religions, including Christians, Muslims, Jews, Hindus, Buddhists, Shinto, believers of religions I have not heard of, and people who don't believe in religions. These people all practice latihan together with no feeling of animosity toward each other. When the latihan begins, thoughts and emotions lose their effectiveness and become cooperative. The phenomena of this world also fall in line as if they have sunken to the margins of consciousness. It is difficult to put into words what it feels like to be in this state. You feel at peace, tranquil and calm. You have a sense of unrestrained freedom; there is nothing to stress about, nor will anything bother you.

This calmness continues to influence and underpin the way members behave toward each other, allowing good relations to be maintained. This sense of calm peacefulness and relaxedness of mind is hard to find elsewhere. It also means that there is less chance of an argument in situations where the topic of conversation would normally generate tension. People of different religions who do latihan together and experience that calm mind are less likely to let these differences be a cause of hostility or conflict with each other. The same applies to people of different tribes, countries, cultures, and languages. In the space of the latihan, these differences cease to be problems.

Inter-faith dialogues are becoming increasingly common around the world. The understanding is that without peace amongst religions, there will be no peace amongst nations, but without dialogues among religions, there will be no peace amongst religions. These efforts are valuable, but they have not yet yielded actual results. It is nearly two hundred years since Beethoven celebrated the words, "All men [will] become brothers," in his Ninth Choral Symphony, and yet we still have no signs of realizing that ideal. Our hearts and minds cause friction amongst us because of differences in opinion. Harmony amongst nations begins with discovering how we can align with the thoughts and emotions of others and where we can compromise. In this respect, the harmony that currently exists as a reality amongst the members of Subud who have overcome differences of opinion and beliefs is surely a first in human history.

When thoughts and emotions are dispersed after latihan, the feeling that remains is a completely new way of relating to one another. When they travel the world, Subud members can do latihan with other Subud members there and feel completely at home with no sense of being in a foreign country. This potential surely means that Subud has the possibility of opening the door to a future of international harmony.

Subud Members' Contributions to Society

Subud actively supports social work by its members. The history of social work in Subud dates back to its very beginning. One of the first enterprises was the establishment of a home for maladjusted boys in the UK in 1960.

Subud members around the world have taken on the challenges of carrying out social work, and these efforts are evident in many countries. These social projects have been initiated by Subud members and receive cooperation from Subud members and groups internationally. This is a significant part of Subud history.

Another example of this is the International Child Development Program (ICDP).

ICDP is a psychosocial program that assists the growth of children from developing countries who have lost their parents through civil wars and are profoundly traumatized. It was set up by a long-time Subud member from Norway, Karsten Hundeide, who is a professor of psychology at Oslo University. First established in Angola, the program spread to countries with intractable conflicts. The program's successes were given academic recognition by the university, and because it was highly praised for its adaptability to many different cultures, the World Health Organization (WHO) selected it for publication as a unique Emotional Health Program.

The focus of the program is not the children so much as the caregivers of that child, whether they be the father, mother, nursery, kindergarten/school teacher, or staff (childcare workers) in institutions. The aim is to improve their quality of care while encouraging the true essence of communication between people. Anyone can be trained in the program regardless of their educational background.

ICDP has already been established in fourteen countries and regions. In recent news, a joint proposal from ICPD and SDIA (see below) was selected from amongst 68,000 applicants around the world for a child assistance project being offered by the Canadian government. The project will receive funding of 200,000 USD for the first eighteen months. This funding will be used to implement an ICDP pilot project and to supply large-scale nutrition to children in a poor region of Peru in South America. ICDP continues to be implemented in many developing countries with support from Subud.

Organization and Operations in Subud

The World Subud Association (WSA), is the umbrella organization for the worldwide Subud community and is made up of the national Subud organizations of all 54 member countries. The WSA is responsible for organizing a World Subud Congress every four years where member countries come together to agree on policy and activities in line with the WSA constitution. Members undertake social projects within various Subud bodies that are affiliated to the WSA. The oldest and most active of these is the charitable wing, Susila Dharma International Association (SDIA), which was founded and incorporated in 1968 in the US. The United Nations recognized the long history of SDIA's social projects around the world and gave it NGO status under the UN so it could take a seat at the UN Economic and Social Council meetings and contribute opinions. SDIA is currently active in twenty-nine countries around the world and supports welfare projects in nineteen of these in America, SE Asia, Africa, and Europe.

Other affiliated Subud associations include SICA, (Subud International Cultural Association) which supports cultural and art-based expression, SYIA (Subud International Youth Association), which supports youth activities, SIHA (Subud International Health Association), which works with health and medical practitioners, and SESI (Subud Enterprise Services International), which supports enterprise activities. These various activities are also promoted by MSF (Muhammad Subuh Foundation), which acts as a financial foundation for Subud in general.

In particular, the cultural wing, SICA, aims to encourage creative expression by its members while developing culture and art through Subud. In the last chapter of *Susila Budhi Dharma*, Bapak says the following:

"… you will soon become adept at doing work that is in tune with your *jiwa* (soul), and this will certainly make your life happy, for this skill will stem or grow from your human *jiwa* (soul), which will have brought to life your whole inner feeling. So it is, my children; hence your zeal for your work will persist and your progress or advance in it will not be disappointing.

That is what is truly called culture, for its source is the human *jiwa* (soul) and it is received in an inner feeling that has risen free from the sway of the ancillary forces. It is a culture filled continuously with the life force. That is why the work you do will be a means for your worship of the Almighty."[9]

APPENDIX A: THE MEANING OF THE NAME SUBUD

Subud is a contraction of the three Sanskrit words, Susila, Budhi, and Dharma. When Subud began to spread, Bapak indicated that this name could be changed if it presented an obstacle to the spread of the latihan. However, no appropriate substitute emerged and the name Subud remained. The meaning of these three words is:

Susila signifies truly human-like behavior and actions.
Budhi signifies the existence of a noble force inside every person that acts as a guiding light to teach us.
Dharma is the attitude of acceptance, trust, submission and surrender to God who created the universe.

Put together, those three words signify that once you submit yourself wholly to the Great Life force of God the creator, the human soul awakens from its sleep so that on this earth, you can live a good life, furnished with the morality appropriate to the human soul, which is the highest being in this world.

Subud is the experience of the spiritual training of the latihan. It is not a teaching nor a creed. A name is needed to exist in this world and the name, 'Subud,' indicates the direction and goal of that spiritual training. Subud members practice the latihan so that they can achieve that goal.

APPENDIX B: THE SUBUD ORGANIZATION AND NETWORK

There are no leaders or hierarchy in Subud. There are no seniors and juniors. All members are equal. All Subud activities around the world are run by the two groups of helpers and committees, which are populated by volunteers.

In most countries, Subud has a national committee that supports all the local groups who, in turn, have local committees. These bodies are responsible for work in the world and are made up of volunteers. They have fixed terms, however, and this is usually for two years. The chief tasks of the committee include registration of members, administrative communications, preparation of latihan spaces, collection and distribution of group information, and determining and running a budget.

The words, "group," "local," "national," and "international" are used in front of the words, "helper" and "committee" to indicate the scope of responsibilities. While the chairperson of the national committee is responsible for managing all worldly affairs, Subud is run as a democracy with the participation of all members. Significant issues are determined at national congresses through deliberation and resolutions.

Helpers are volunteers who take care of the spiritual work. They become helpers after many years of experience of the latihan and there is no fixed term. Their chief duties are:

- Explaining Subud to applicants and new members
- Opening new members
- Looking after group latihans
- Helping members in need of advice
- Supporting community work

Helpers have the important role of acting as the face of Subud, but as there is no hierarchy in Subud, helpers do not have authority nor are they considered better than anyone else. Only God can know the spiritual state of members, and it is quite possible that the spiritual state of a newly opened member is at a higher stage than that of a helper with many years of experience.

Varindra Vittachi was an internationally well-known journalist, a regular columnist for Newsweek magazine, director of information of the United Nations Population Fund, executive of UNICEF and the first chairperson of the Subud World Association. He described the organization of Subud as a rarity in the world, as there was responsibility but no authority at any level. At every event in Subud, there can be no such thing as a unilateral decision. Varindra's words were meant in admiration but it is not an easy feat to steer a group in Subud when not even the chairperson has the right to push their opinion and all decisions must be made through patient discussions with all members to reach a consensus. In Subud, if a consensus cannot be reached, either the decision is postponed or, if all members agree, it is decided through testing.

Subud does not charge fixed fees but runs on the voluntary donations of its members. Members who alone determine how much they are able to donate to their local and national Subud groups, cover all the costs of maintaining latihan spaces, producing and distributing regular newsletters, and the budget for maintaining and developing the organization.

EPILOGUE

I have dealt with the main features of Subud, but actually, it is not possible to describe the latihan itself in words. Therefore, I feel that I have written merely a part of the overall picture of Subud, somewhat like the blind man feeling the elephant's ear in the proverb and thinking that it represented the whole creature.

Bapak once said that if we were to describe the latihan in words, it would take a very long time and a very large number of pages. No matter how hard we pick our brains, the latihan of Subud simply will not fit within the framework of our normal consciousness. Even the manner in which it appeared is outside ordinary human understanding. We cannot comprehend Subud with our hearts and minds. Nor is there anything in the past that we can compared it to. The latihan is the core of Subud, and yet the latihan itself has many strange features that our everyday consciousness simply cannot even imagine. The way that things change and are produced by the latihan is the same as the way nature transforms and creates things. There is no advance notice or explanation; what happens, happens.

In addition, the latihan of Subud comes from a new knowledge and awareness that had not existed before; firstly, this is the understanding of the nature and limitations of the heart and mind, and secondly, there is the issue of acquiring a spiritual body for life after death. Currently, these are the facts as indicated by Bapak, but to borrow scientific terms, they are still at the hypothetical stage and have not yet been proven through observation and experimentation. Yet, these hypotheses provide a reasonable explanation for the many mysteries of our relationship to the spiritual world. Even scientific hypotheses that are difficult to prove are seen as being close to established theory if they succeed in providing a reasonable explanation of existing facts. Therefore, it is possible that the content of Bapak's hypotheses, should they prove to hold more truth than hypothetical foundations, will have a major impact on our understanding of the universe.

Looking back, it is exactly sixty-four years ago that I first heard about Subud. In fact, when I was a student at university, without any warning, I had an unexpected experience where I witnessed the power of God. Through this, I became convinced of the God who created and maintains this universe and supports the activities within it. I had a great desire to repeat this experience. If I had not had this experience, it is very likely that I would have not had any interest nor would I have been opened in this tiny group called Subud, with no more than 300 members that nobody knew about and that was founded in Indonesia. There were certainly many reasons to be doubtful.

The more you continue diligently with the latihan, and the more you totally submit, the more your understanding of Subud will widen, deepen, and approach the truth. As long as you continue with the latihan, your spiritual progress will not stop, regardless of your age. This is the wonderful nature of the latihan. We cannot experience or know everything of Subud. The Great Life that we come into contact with in the latihan is from God, and to know everything of Subud suggests to know and experience everything of God, which is an impossibility.

In this book, I mentioned that only Bapak had traveled the full spiritual journey of Subud, but to be more accurate, it is not possible for a human being to experience the whole of Subud. However, I do think that while one person cannot experience the whole of Subud, as present and future Subud members continue to ponder the nature and value of Subud, the vast potential of it will become abundantly clear. Even if we cannot experience the whole of the power of God, we can at least draw closer to Him. As long as our progress does not stop, there is no end to how close we can come, even if it takes an infinity.

Bapak wished that through the latihan, Subud members could experience something akin to what he experienced, even if it was not identical, and therefore be able to endorse his words. Based on my own experiences, this is something I anticipate because the search for the possibilities opened up by the latihan has just begun and true understanding will follow.

Ten years ago, I set down the spiritual experiences that I had had in my latihan that were particularly strong and unusual in a book that was published both in English and Japanese (Subud – A Spiritual Journey. Booksurge Publishing). In that book, I kept my explanation of the substance of Subud to a minimum; I was worried that I would not be able to write generally about Subud. I am still of that opinion, however, this book is an attempt to give shape to something that can fill that space.

Bapak said that we could understand the true benefits of the latihan after we die. This is because while our lifespan is limited to around one hundred years at most, our soul will live on for an eternity after we die. However, it does not stop there; the blessings of the latihan go beyond that of an individual member and affect their ancestors and their descendants. Many members have reported that they have experienced that their parents or ancestors have benefited from their own latihan.

Bapak said that the latihan was a gift from God to humankind and whether it spread around the world or not, was up to the will of God. He also said that Subud should not be spread through advertising or invitation, but through others recognizing the benefits it brings. The only way is for people to experience the latihan for themselves, evaluate, and judge it based on their own experiences. To embark on such a journey requires a big commitment. Perhaps the time for Subud to be appreciated by society is still in the future.

In writing this book, I have tried to get close to describing an overall picture of Subud, and despite the risks and my own lack of ability, I hope that it goes some way to bringing that future a little closer.

REFERENCE LIST

1. Sumohadiwidjojo, M. S. (1990. P34) *Autobiography*. UK: Subud Publications International Ltd.
2. Lyle, R. (1983). *Subud*. Kent, England: Humanus Limited.
3. Holy Bible, New Living Translation, copyright © 1996, 2004, 2015 by Tyndale House Foundation. Used by permission of Tyndale House Publishers, Inc., Carol Stream, Illinois 60188. All rights reserved.
4. NKH Special Series, THE BODY, Miracles of Our Inner Social Networks, Prologue: Our Talkative Body Organs 30/09/2017
5. Sumohadiwidjojo, M. S. (1991, p.1) *Susila Budhi Dharma* E Sussex, England: Subud Publications International Ltd.
6. Sumohadiwidjojo, M. S. (1991, p.10) *Susila Budhi Dharma*. E Sussex, England: Subud Publications International Ltd.
7. Holy Bible, NEW INTERNATIONAL READER'S VERSION®. Copyright © 1996, 1998 Biblica. All rights reserved throughout the world. Used by permission of Biblica.
8. Sumohadiwidjojo, M. S. (1960) *The Meaning of Subud*. 59 LON 1, PI, London: The Subud Brotherhood in England
9. Vittachi, V. (1988) *Bouquets for Bapak A Memoir of Subud*. E Sussex, England: Subud Publications International Ltd.
10. Sumohadiwidjojo, M. S. (1991, p.122) *Susila Budhi Dharma* E Sussex, England: Subud Publications International Ltd.

Printed in the United States
By Bookmasters